A
PHENOMENALLY PHRANK
HISTORY
OF
PHILOSOPHY

Anyone born in Luton is bound to enquire into the meaning of life. JOHN FARMAN is no exception, and when his parents left home he devoted what remained of his time on earth to questions like "Who am I?" and "Where did they go?"

Educated at Harrow (School of Art) and the Royal College of Art, he pursued (but rarely caught up with) a career as an illustrator before plugging in a word processor and stumbling into writing. The rest is history (see over).

John Farman

A
PHENOMENALLY PHRANK
HISTORY
OF
PHILOSOPHY

(without the poncy bits)

MACMILLAN

First published 1996 by
Macmillan Children's Books
a division of Macmillan Publishers Ltd
25 Eccleston Place, London SW1W 9NF
and Basingstoke

Associated companies throughout the world

ISBN 0 330 34555 9

Text and illustrations copyright © John Farman 1996

3 5 7 9 8 6 4 2

A CIP catalogue record for this book is available from the British Library.

Printed by Mackays of Chatham PLC, Chatham, Kent.

The publishers would like to thank Joyce Johnson for permission
to reprint the limerick on page 21 of this book. It was originally
published in *The Penguin Book of Limericks* © E.O. Parrot 1983.

All possible care has been taken to trace the ownership of every
limerick included and to make full acknowledgement for its use.
If any errors have accidentally occurred, they will be corrected
in subsequent editions, provided notification is sent to the publishers.

To the late
Bertrand Russell,
who once referred to me thus,
'Who?'

Contents

Introduction

Imagine being told by your mum and dad that if you went off in a boat and forgot to turn right or left, you would eventually fall off the world. Imagine thinking that the world was only 60,000 years old (instead of the 4,500,000,000 it really is). But these are problems of *science*, and let's face it, early man had enough to think about simply keeping his head above water in a horribly hostile world.

What about the bigger questions like: what is man? why is he here? how does he figure in the whole scheme of things? who is God? does He even exist? and what is this strange new thing called thinking? Science can be relatively simple to pursue, as through investigation and experimentation certain truths can be arrived at, but thought (or thinking about thought) is much more complicated and far less easy to get your head around.

This little book attempts to explain, in simple language, how our thinking shuddered forwards, sideways and often backwards from the earliest times, in an effort to sort it all out. The proper term for this is a word that makes most

people roll their eyes and change the subject *tout de suite* ...
PHILOSOPHY! If you're worried because you know absolutely nothing about the subject and feel somewhat ignorant – fear not. Before I was asked to write this mighty work, I could write all I knew about the history of philosophical thought in the margin of *Beano.*

But, as my publishers know, I'll try anything once, and so I edged on to the yellow brick road leading to supreme philosophical enlightenment in fear and trepidation (with the almost certain knowledge that I'd be bored out of my skull, and would end up with thousands of copies of *A Phenomenally Phrank History of Philosophy* in my mum's garage). Oddly enough, I actually found the subject really fascinating and somewhat wacky, once I'd managed to decipher all the obscure jargon and quasi-intellectual bull that experts always seem to use to justify their existence, and once I'd been put on to the brilliant late S. E. Frost Jnr's *Basic Teachings of the Great Philosophers.*

WHAT IS MAN?

WHY IS HE HERE?

HOW DOES HE FIGURE IN THE WHOLE SCHEME
OF THINGS?

WHO IS GOD?

DOES HE EVEN EXIST?

AND WHAT IS THIS STRANGE NEW THING CALLED

... THINKING?

CHAPTER I

. . . .

In the Beginning

The dictionary definition of philosophy reads: *'the rational investigation of being, knowledge and right conduct.'* I prefer to call it *'talking about thinking (about thinking)'* (I think!).

When I was a kid, like many kids before me, Eric* and I used to stare out through my bedroom window on starry nights wondering where all that twinkly blackness stopped and when and how the universe started. In those days I wanted to believe everything my mum and dad told me, but being an awkward little varmint (now an awkward *big* varmint) I soon became suspicious. At Sunday school I was introduced to the first bit of Genesis, which describes how God set about his greatest task (see Chapter 10) of creating the world and all its auxiliary bits and pieces.

But, as I said before, I was a difficult child, much to the dismay of my parents, and had a hard time believing in fairies,

*my bear

ghosts or even Father Christmas (I always clocked that it was my dad in that daft white beard and carpet slippers), so obviously I had a bit of a problem with this little tale. Did God *really* decide to have a bit of fun and create a universe with the earth somewhere in the middle? If so, I reasoned, what had He been doing before that? Once He'd mapped out the general plan, did He really make a vast list of everything He wanted on it – from peanuts to pigs and dahlias to dinosaurs? If so, why stop there? And man? What was He thinking of when he made us? Having gone to all the trouble to create something that can think for itself, and achieve a technology to improve its lot so dramatically, how come God fashioned a species also capable of cruelly slaying its mates in such huge numbers, destroying its own environment and producing TV programmes like *The Big Breakfast* or *Come Dancing*?

This version of 'the start of it all' just didn't ring true (and I suppose it was this same lack of belief in everything they were ever told that spurred on those early philosophers from the beginnings of civilization). What if there isn't a God? I pondered. What if our world and universe are just pure chance? What if there *is* no bigger plan? What if what we see is what we get? What if this is IT! I felt very lonely (and so did Eric).

Ever since our forefathers first started scribbling their thoughts down, us humans have kept records of our attempts to understand how and why we are here. Most times the theories turned into legend or religion, and were passed down from scribe to scribe and priest to priest like Chinese whispers.

Some early civilizations, like those of the Egyptians and the Babylonians, ran for thousands of years making up their gods and beliefs as they went along. The grumpy Egyptians had been obsessed by death, believing that their souls would eventually descend to the fiery underground to be met and judged by a chap called *Osiris* who grilled them (in more ways than one) about what they'd been up to on earth. It wasn't a one-way ticket, however, as they thought that at some stage the soul returned to the body. That's why the Egyptian kings got their slaves to mummify their bodies and build such fab tombs – so that the travel-weary soul would have something nice and snug to look forward to on its return.

Babylonian religion was far more sensible, being more concerned with having a good time in this world without trying to sort out the next. They were deeply into magic, astrology and the supernatural and they can be blamed for its spread throughout the ancient world (and the likes of Russell Grant and Mystic Meg).

We all know about Greek art and writing (all those saucy gods, daft myths etc.), and most of us know that they invented maths and science (and the stuffed vine leaf) but it was in the realms of intellectual thinking that they get top score. Christianity was only a twinkle in God's eye at this time, as his best boy Jesus's birth was well over five centuries away. Without the concept of a single all-seeing, all-knowing, all-everythinging god (like ours), they felt quite happy to guess at the nature of the world without the fear of treading heavily on theological toes. It was this that gave them the ability, for the first time in history, to set learning free from the ball and chain of religion and make their civilization as great and memorable as it turned out to be.

So the early Greek philosophers set about trying to sort out their version of the nature of the universe, and started by asking a simple question: what's the 'stuff' that everything comes from? They were determined to try to write down their conclusions rationally and truthfully without constantly diving back into the labyrinth of myth and legend.

The first person to tell anyone what he thought, or should I say, the first person that anyone remembered talking about what he thought, was a certain **Thales of Miletus** who lived around 585 BC. If, when you've struggled through this book, you're looking for someone to blame for the beginnings of all this philosophical stuff, this is your man. Thales was a wheeler-dealer in the Greek olive oil business and registered clever-person, who seemed to have gained his enviable place in history by a) predicting a total eclipse and b) claiming that everything, including himself, came from water (as opposed to olive oil?). A lifetime's work? Maybe not. To be fair, he'd observed water turning to ice and back again and, when heated, becoming steam (and then returning to water) so therefore surmised that if it could be 'hard' and 'soft' there was a fair chance that all things from boulders to belly dancers came from and, much later, returned to good old H_2O. His reward in history for all his work was the title of 'one of the seven wise men of Greece'. (I'm surprised there's that many!)

So, if that was the beginning of philosophy – what was the big deal, you might ask? But human (or should I say Greek) nature being what it is (or was), someone soon came along to say something completely different.

Anaximander (610–550 BC), another local boy, reckoned that Thales was well off the ball (or boil) with his rather wet theory, and claimed that everything in the universe came from one extremely large living mass called *the boundless* which turned out to be slime. (Boundless slime? Yuk!) Everything except, I'm glad to report, humans – who came from ... something else. This something else turned out to be some sort of fish, though he didn't specify the precise species. Our world, he claimed, was cylindrical at the centre of the universe and not supported by anything. Nice try, Anaximander, but ... WRONG!

Miletus seems to have been a place where people liked to sit around pondering the big questions, and the next guy, **Anaximenes** (570–510 BC), was a student of Anaximander, and said the others were both barking up the wrong tree (or simply barking). He swore blind that because all animals and men breathed air, that air must have at some stage turned into flesh, bone and blood and therefore wind, clouds, water, earth and stone. There also had been some whisperings to the effect that the world might be spherical but Anaximenes thought we lived on a sort of a desert island disc cast adrift in space, otherwise surely all those people not living on the very top bit would fall off (gravity hadn't been invented yet).

5

This **Miletian** school was important, not for *what* it achieved, but what it really *tried* to achieve. The theories of Thales and Co., which hardly show any hint of human desires or moral ideas, should be seen merely as scientific speculations. The questions they asked were good. OK, the answers were a bit off-line but who cares, they spurred on a whole host of questioners for truth. It's interesting to note that at this time the poor Brits were too busy being conquered by the crude Celts to think about *anything* else – and were more worried about whether they had a future than where they'd come from!

No way, said **Heraclitus**, known as 'the riddler' (pre-Batman), in 520 BC, in answer to the Miletians' ramblings. He too was really anxious to get in on the 'what's it all about' act. Because everything in the universe is constantly changing, he conjectured (dodgily), it must be made of fire. Why? Because fire's always changing (wow!). When he delivered his gob smacking truth – 'you can't step in the same river twice' (as both *you* and *it* were always changing) – he seemed to assume that, as theories go, it was game, set and match. Heraclitus was also rather big on opposites, proclaiming, for instance, that if you never felt ill, you'd never know what it was like to be well or that, if you'd never been cold you'd never know what it was like to be warm. Does that mean that unless you'd been tall, you'd never know what it was like to be short? Keep riddlin', Heraclitus!

Rubbish, said **Pythagoras** (him of right-angled triangle fame) a little later. If everything, including musical notation, can be measured, and physical natures receive an understandable grounding in different geometric structures, it must mean that *numbers* were the 'stuff' that the cosmos was made of. Pythagoras' other great contribution to modern philosophical thought was that you shouldn't eat animals or beans because they had souls. He even set up a society which involved total silence (*Silence of the Beans?*) and various taboos including, I suppose, the protection of the aforementioned beans. I take it a certain Mr Heinz was *not* of the same opinion. Pythagoras believed in reincarnation and claimed to remember former lives (as a bean?). Our soul, which is a god in itself (that's nice) could once have been an animal or a plant and could break free from us by a religious dedication to study before rejoining all its soulmates in the universal world.

You're *all* a bit right, said **Empedocles** (490–430 BC) the famous poet, orator, scientist, statesman, miracle worker and freelance self-styled god, but you're all a bit wrong too. The universe is made up of air, earth, fire and water (and bullsh...?) in tiny little particles, mixing and separating under the influence of Love and Hate. Everything in the universe is alive and has the ability to think. Humans, luckily, have more of this power, though we can all think of a few specimens that would disprove this (Keith Chegwyn for one). Empedocles agreed with Pythagoras that souls are immortal, adding that they are destined to an eternal cycle of birth and rebirth owing to their annoying habit of every so often falling from heavenly grace.

The good folk of Acragas, where Empedocles lived,

thought all this philosophizing was ever so clever and, flushed with success, he took himself to the brink of a volcano called Mount Edna (or was it Etna?) and threw himself in, convinced that he could prove at last that he was a *proper* god and therefore invulnerable. Unfortunately he *wasn't* and he *wasn't*.

From around 500 BC a group of philosophers called the **Eleats**, from Elea in Southern Italy, began to make themselves heard. The best one was a guy called **Parmenides** (born in 510 BC) who seemed to do all his philosophy in verse form:

> There was young lady from Turkey,
> Who thought she would ... etc.

Apparently, in one ditty, he told of some local goddess who reckoned that 'reality must necessarily be, or must necessarily not be, or must both be and not be'. Ah yes, that's very clear, your goddesship! What she really meant was that there was only one 'Thing' and that was big, round, changeless, imperishable, indivisible, perfect and motionless, and that anything that appears to change, or didn't fulfil all those criteria, must be an illusion. Parmenides thought that nothing could come out of nothing (which certainly relates to the interest on my bank balance).

He and his fellow Eleats disappeared so far up their own ... er, universes that they ended up not even trusting what they actually saw themselves, believing that their senses were giving them a bum deal. This way of thinking became known as *rationalism*.

Anaxagoras (499–428 BC) was the guy who suggested

that the sun was a white hot lump of stone even bigger than the whole Pelopponese (the southern part of Greece) and was exiled for being silly. His other famous 'thought' was that there is a portion of everything in everything else ... except mind. This, he explained, meant that whatever something changes into is in some way already in it before it changes (transvestites take note). He also insisted that matter could theoretically be divided and subdivided for ever and ever.

It's safe to say that by this time the early Greek philosophers had got themselves into a fine old pickle. Some thought everything was part of everything else; some thought everyone was made of slime; some thought nothing stays the same for more than five minutes, and some thought the universe was made out of anything from fire to numbers etc, etc. Luckily, in the nick of time (around 400 BC) a chap called **Democritus** hit the headlines.

Nicknamed 'the laughing philosopher' he was an odd guy by all accounts: in order to keep laughing he blinded himself. Certainly not normal behaviour, though it must be said there was a certain logic (albeit Greek) behind it. Apparently he fancied so many members of the opposite sex that it was making him miserable (know the feeling?). So much so, that he thought if he couldn't actually *see* them the problem would go away. Dramatic, but presumably effective. (Actually if he'd carried on the way he was going, he'd probably have gone blind anyway.)

Anyway, back to the plot. Democritus went along with earlier ideas that developments in nature didn't necessarily mean that anything had actually 'changed' (see Parmenides). He reckoned instead that everything in the universe was made out of loads and loads of tiny little invisible 'bits' which he called *atoms* (*atom* means 'uncuttable'). These little chaps were constantly whizzing about in space covered with little hooks (pre-Velcro). Every now and again a bunch of them would stick together and make something. Anything from a great dictator to a humble porker could be formed from these lumps of atoms. When the aforementioned dictator or pig died all the atoms would agree to go their different ways and fly off into space to see what else they could make. Let's look at it another way. If you were to catch all the atoms that went to make the newly deceased pig and put them in a box, and then shook these pig particles about a bit, what would come out when you opened the lid would not necessarily be a reconstituted porker, but could be almost anything (sausages even).

Democritus was nearly right. Modern atomic theory agrees that everything in nature is composed of atoms that have a habit of joining together and breaking apart. This means that an atom that was once part of, say, a pig's snout, could just as easily have joined up with a bunch of his fascist mates and become Adolf Hitler's horrid little moustache.

Unlike many of the philosophers before him, he didn't believe that any exterior force (gods etc.) helped this ongoing process. He did believe, however, in the human soul and that that too was made of atoms, albeit better quality ones. (Try finding that in modern atomic theory!)

All the Greek 'thinkers' had thought that man was just a

part of the universe, and made up of all the same bits and pieces as everything else, only more refined. The **Sophists** (Greek for 'expert'), just to be different, saw man as the centre of the universe, and 'the measure of all things' – a concept that is becoming very popular again. They tore him away from the inevitability of natural law and made him the master of his own fate.

One of the most famous Sophists was a chap called **Aristippus** (*c*.435–356 BC). His aim in life was to gain as much pleasure as possible, but he said he didn't want to be a slave to it – he wanted to be in charge. When talking about his upmarket girlfriend, Lais, he said, 'I have Lais, she not me', which sums up every chauvinist remark ever uttered. In other words, it doesn't matter about the pleasure of the 'receiver', as long as the 'doer' gets maximum buzz.

Socrates (470–399 BC) agreed with the Sophists by showing two fingers to the problems of the universe, preferring to concentrate on his own and those of his fellow man. At the same time, he sneered at the Sophists because they did all their philosophizing for cash, whereas he taught purely as 'one who loves wisdom' (and private incomes). He was one of the first internationally recognized ever-so-clever people, one of the reasons being that he never wrote anything down, but relied on those non-paying punters whose ears he borrowed to tell everyone else. He actually sounds rather infuriating, as his method of work involved strolling around the main squares of Athens, pretending to be stupid, and asking innocent bystanders interminable questions, without ever actually answering theirs. (Don't people like that get up your nose?) By pretending that he knew nothing, he let people constantly ramble on, putting their own sandalled feet in it, until certain truths emerged as by products of their ignorance.

But why was Socrates so important? What did he say that made him a household name for centuries? Socrates was probably the first person on the records to move away from Science with a big S . . . What's the earth made of? Where are we in relation to the sun? etc. He started asking questions like: Is there a basic principle of right or wrong? What is the highest goal by which everything else is measured? He came up with a one word answer – KNOWLEDGE.

Working on the slightly dodgy assumption that no one actually tries to be bad, he went on to say that all you need to know is whether something is good or not, and then (obviously) go for the good. Therefore, the most important endeavour of man should be to actually discover all that is good (chocolate chip ice cream?), and if he devotes his life to this it will make him a jolly good chap (or chappess). As an added bonus, he reckoned that this good man could, through this knowledge of good and bad, actually influence his destiny, both here on earth and wherever he happens to end up afterwards. This, for the first time, implied that we, as humans, have an element of choice as to what happens to us. According to old Socrates, if a man turns into a bounder and a rotter, it's his choice (albeit the wrong one) – so hard cheese!

His 'divine voice' (as he called it) really got up the Athenians' noses and eventually, when they'd had enough, they accused him of 'introducing new gods and corrupting the youth' (poor youth). He was found guilty as charged and made to drink hemlock, which shut him up for good. All the later Greek schools of philosophy, however, reckoned they owed it all to Socrates – except for the Epicureans (see p.23) who called him the 'Athenian buffoon'.

Socrates' chief groupie was **Plato** (427–347 BC) a rich kid who (post-hemlock), jotted down so much of what his mentor said and what *he* personally thought of what he said, that no one could be quite sure where Socrates ended and Plato began. As Socrates was such an unpleasant so-and-so (and ugly to boot) we'll give Plato the benefit of the doubt and credit *all* the following stuff to him.

Plato wasn't such a wise-guy as Socrates. He tried to drive some middle path between the Sophists and all the miscellaneous odds and ends the early Greeks had scribbled down when they were bumping around, trying to work out where man fitted in the universe. Plato reckoned that *man* is the measure of all things because, like it or not, certain universal principles, notions, concepts or ideas are already in him (like the operating system in a computer). The real universe is simply a series of pure changeless ideas which man can grasp and, in grasping them, grasp reality, thereby answering the big question – WHAT'S IT ALL ABOUT? Man, you'll be pleased to know, was different to animals, who Plato reckoned were soulless and thick, despite being made in the same 'factory'.

The Sophists had thought that concepts like right or wrong varied from place to place, i.e. what may be dead naughty in Manchester might be a bit of a laugh in London. Socrates, on the other hand, had said that there were absolute rules about *everything*, wherever one lived and in whatever time span. Plato went further by saying that concepts like right or wrong were not only eternal and unchanging regarding us lot (the human race) but were also eternal and unchanging in nature.

The world of the senses (sight, touch, hearing, smell and taste), he said, is always changing and therefore unreal; this is BAD. The world of ideas is pure and unchanging; this is GOOD. Men (and women) can only know the real world through reason: reason is therefore the highest GOOD for humanity. The aim of life should be for the soul to part company (amicably) with the body it's been living in, so that it can get stuck into the *real* world of ideas (bodies not required).

But Plato also said that reason is only a part of a man's life (even though it's the only bit that distinguishes him from also-rans like monkeys). He also has emotional feelings, desires and appetites (I feel I desire some lunch ...). A 'good' life is one where they all live side by side happily, but with reason being in charge. Well, that's what Plato reckoned.

He was always going on about how much all natural phenomena were alike, believing that ordinary everyday objects like tables, chairs, flowers (or pop-up toasters for that matter), are merely poor copies of perfect forms. Of these there were only a limited number and they were stored in that cosmic (not Comet) warehouse in the sky — Heaven. On the other shelves are forms for abstract items like beauty, good-ness, truth, love and soul music, and nasty things like badness

14

(and baldness), ugliness, spots and game-show hosts. These forms or ideas exist like moulds and everything we see around us is to some degree an imperfect replica. (Can you imagine a *more* imperfect game-show host?) Art, he wouldn't have in the house for obvious reasons: he saw it as merely a replica of a replica. First, the flower-mould on the heavenly shelf, then the flower in your garden, then the painting of it.

CHAPTER 2

··

And then there was ... Aristotle

Things were really hotting up in the world of philosophy when a doctor's son, **Aristotle-of-Stagira** (somewhere in Macedonia, *c.*435–356 BC), was to soar higher than even Plato in the 'Best Philosopher Ever' stakes. Actually, I think this rather cheeky remark sums up what he thought of the master: *'Plato is dear to me, but dearer still is truth.'*

When only seventeen, and probably sporting hundreds of GCSEs, he joined Plato's flash science 'Academy' in Athens where he was first a student and then a teacher. When Plato finally went to heaven (or wherever current thinking reckoned one ended up) Aristotle quit the school and went to work for Philip of Macedon (king) as tutor to his son, Alexander, who his dad had 'Great' plans for. After achieving this no mean feat, Aristotle returned to Athens to found his own school – the *Lyceum* (home of natural philosophy and ballroom dancing) – and have a jolly good think.

Aristotle was happy to admit that 'ideas' existed and so did 'matter' (for that matter).

But he wouldn't have it that they were separate things. Ideas (or 'forms' as he called them) were not floating around willynilly (or stuck on shelves in heaven!), but were actually *in* things — *all* things in fact. Form and matter, he said, couldn't be separated and should always, therefore, stay together eternally. So, instead of trundling along his predecessor Plato's line that everything around us is a copy of a perfect 'form', Aristotle preferred to think that what you see is effectively what you get — or vice versa.

Example: Pick a pip ... any pip. Let's say an apple pip. We recognize the 'form' of your average apple pip as being the same as every other apple pip. Although this pip is a particular pip, we must never separate the *form* 'pip' from it. But this pip is not just a form, it has actual *matter*. In order for our precious personal pip to exist, it *must* realize itself in matter, and the more perfect it is, the more perfectly the form is realized (phew!). Now, the pip in our hand, though presumably happy being a mere pip (matter-wise) has another form it wouldn't mind being ... a tree, or more specifically ... an apple tree.

So, we plant this pip and it strives for tree-dom. End of story? Not quite. The resulting tree could, if unlucky, be then cut down and made into anything from pipe-racks to carved apples. Here the apple tree is 'matter' and this particular carved apple (for instance) is the form that the tree seeks to realize. In every case — the pip, the tree, the wooden apple — there is matter and form. At all the various stages the object which exists is both the realization of the form and also the right matter needed to reach the form it wants to become next. Therefore (at long last), ideas or forms never change.

18

The form 'pip' will always be 'pip' and never 'tree' and so on and so on (and so on). Matter, Aristotle concluded, is always taking on new forms. This continual striving of matter to create new forms became the guts of our Aristotle's explanation of the universe. Wow!

Everything in the universe, he claimed, had its place. Why do fish swim in water? Why do birds fly in the sky? Why do apples fall to the ground? Why do fools fall in love? All these questions he answered with one simple, get-home-early reply – *because it's their nature*. So there!!

When he wasn't busy making profound statements about the universe, Aristotle invented logic, semantics, biological taxonomy, the hula hoop and the philosophy of science*. On a slightly more dodgy note, he proclaimed that women were simply 'unfinished men', being merely passive and receptive (certainly not my experience, Aristotle!). All they were good for was receiving and nurturing the seed from us men who unselfishly, and through the goodness of our hearts, passed on all the child's characteristics through our sperm. In other Aristotelian words, girls, we lads provide the 'form', and you merely the soil or 'substance' to grow it in. This view, I'm afraid to report, was held throughout most of the Middle Ages (see following chapter). Now I wonder if there are any women of a feminist disposition out there who've got anything to say about that?

*Spot the odd one out.

19

We are now approaching the end of the fourth century BC and we can lump together everything that has gone before under the term *Natural Philosophy*. Athens was, however, beginning to lose its role as top place philosophy-wise, largely due to the antics of Aristotle's former pupil, young Alexander, who'd been flexing his 'Greatness', conquering everything he could lay his hands on. This drew the whole Eastern or Oriental world together with the Greek civilization for three hundred years. This Greek-dominated culture – which encompassed Macedonia, Syria and Egypt – is called **Hellenism**, probably because it was pure hell if you weren't actually Greek … or Roman, as it turned out.

In 50 BC Rome and the Romans became top dog in all matters political and, more to the point, military, having, up to that time, simply been a part of Greek culture. Luckily, though the Greeks were well out of the picture on the old control stakes, their philosophy and culture lived on (with a few Oriental gods thrown in), probably because the Romans (a bit tardy in the thinking department) couldn't be bothered to invent one of their own (and were far more interested in conquering and partying). *Death* was very much the buzzword in those days, and philosophers were only brought in to see if they could shed any light on the people's fears. To this end, religion and philosophy joined together and patched up their differences.

It's safe to say that Hellenic philosophy was all about, and only about, *how* men should live and, following that, *how* they should die. Ethics (or morals) was the name of the game, and the following were the four directions

20

philosophers took to try and investigate it:

The **Cynics** (400 BC) were nicknamed the dog philosophers, probably after their main-man **DiOGenes** (actually known as 'the dog'), whose shameless habits certainly left a lot to be desired. The Cynics reckoned that desire for anything beyond the minimal bodily satisfactions should be condemned as unnatural. So, for the Cynics, a virtuous life consisted of an independence achieved by mastery over their desires and needs (no fun involved). Diogenes, for instance, to set a good example, lived in a kennel-like barrel (detached), with only his cloak, stick, bread-bag and microwave oven (not really), practising what he preached and often abusing himself in a most disgusting manner (use your imagination) in the main squares of Athens simply to prove how easily one's sexual desires can be satisfied. He was once sitting happily in his barrel when the great Alexander walked up and asked how he was doing. This, apparently, was the result:

> Simple living was clearly the nub
> Of the teaching of one who could snub
> Alexander the Great
> With: 'Move along, mate!
> You are taking the sun off my tub.'
>
> JOYCE JOHNSON

The Cynics, bless 'em, weren't the least bit worried about falling ill, claiming that suffering and death were all in a life's work, which was just as well for old Diogenes who keeled over after eating some certainly not harmless (or armless) octopus.

The founder of the **Stoics** (300 BC) was a tall, good-looking Cypriot guy called **Zeno** (sounds like cough mixture) who joined up with the Cynics in Athens having been shipwrecked (which was enough to make anyone cynical). Zeno's version of their philosophy was called **Stoicism** because he used to lecture his students under a portico – which is *stoa* in Greek (see Fairly Daft Reasons For Naming Anything). They, too, were obsessed with the problems involved in achieving a good life. They liked old Aristotle's 'form' (or 'force') and 'matter' theory – force does the moving while matter has to take what's coming to it. Plato taught that they are not separate, but both live happily together in every object. The Stoics thought they were *both* actual bodies – force being fine-grained, and matter – coarse and formless (like me?). All these forces get together (on Friday nights?) and form a jolly *big* force which becomes the active soul of the universe. They thought that this must be in fire form and that the resulting heat made and moved everything. Haven't we heard that somewhere before? (See Heraclitus.)

This fire, they went on, is connected to everything in the universe, just as the soul of man is related to his body. Out of this fire, they reckoned, air, water and earth combine to make everything from stars to strawberry ice cream (my words, not theirs). This divine principle flows through every object in the universe, bringing it life. For them the universe was a huge perfect ball bobbing around in space, held together by its soul (God?).

But the Stoics were a weird lot, saying that sickness and death were all part of life's rich pattern, following unbreakable laws of nature. Therefore, there was no such thing as an accident, which meant that when something slightly tedious like death did come knocking at your door, you simply let it in, sat it down, and then got on with it. And if you're feeling a little poorly:

Said the Stoic, tormented by gout:
'There are times when I'm tempted to doubt
Our pose about pain
And disposed to complain
It is something we're better without.'

THOMAS THORNELEY

Back to Zeno, whose famous paradoxes shot down most existing theories of motion. Take the flying arrow paradox. If you shoot an arrow into the sky, at every moment in its flight that arrow occupies a space equal to its own length. But for anything to occupy a space equal to its own length is equivalent to its being at rest. Therefore the arrow is at rest at every moment of its flight (try telling that to a dead cowboy).

If you liked the Cynics, you'll simply adore the **Epicureans**. The idea came from one of Socrates' pupils called Aristippus (p.11) who suggested that the highest aim in life was to enjoy oneself (I'll drink to that); that pleasure was the highest good and pain the worstest evil.

Later on, **Epicurus** (341–270 BC) decided to

23

cobble together Aristippus' theories on pleasure with Democritus' theories about atoms. He and his fellow Epicureans made their home in his back garden in Athens and offered a jolly good time to anyone who came in. They warned, however, that too much pleasure could bring nasty side effects (as can be witnessed outside *The Ferret and Brown Trousers* on Saturday nights) and this should be taken into consideration. Not all pleasures are sensual, however, and the love of art and friendship are often just as worthy (but not nearly so much fun). Death, they claimed, was a doddle. Epicurus had told them, somewhat simplistically, that as long as they lived, death was not to be seen, and when it eventually caught up with them, they were no longer around to see it anyway. Just as well, seeing as he died on the lavatory!! He loved old Democritus' 'soul atoms' idea because it involved none of that life-after-death malarkey. When we die, he had claimed, our 'soul atoms' realize they're flogging a dead horse (or hearse) and disappear fairly smartish.

Where society was concerned, Epicurus' pronouncements could be said to be self-defeating. His attitude was that the *wise* man could be well advised to avoid marriage and children, as they were a great 'disturbance' (and that's without mothers-in-law!). This leads one to wonder what he might put in its place – unless he only thought it advisable for idiots to marry.

The world was getting perilously close to the end of the pre-Christian era and men were actually searching for new religions to comfort them. Thanks to all the totally wacky and always confusing teachings of the large proportion of the

24

philosophers that had gone before, your average man in the toga was feeling as perplexed as a kid at a pick'n'mix sweet counter.

At around this time, a Jewish gentlemen living in Alexandria (Egypt) called **Philo** (160–80 BC) let it be known that he rated God way above anything that ever existed or any idea that had gone before. God, he said, was the source of all good, and matter the source of all evil. Likewise in man, his spiritual side was good, while his body (or matter) was the seat of all evil (especially after a curry). There were many powers (or spirits), he said, that radiated from God; one of which was called *Logos*, whose part-time job had been to create the world or universe, under the close direction of his boss (God). Everything Logos made was a copy of an idea in God's mind (a bit like Plato's 'perfect-form-on-a-shelf' wheeze). In fact, it could be said Philo was trying to get old Plato's philosophy into bed with the Jewish religion.

Time for another 'ism'. The next one to come along, unlike the past three which were inspired by Socrates and, like buses, all going to end up in more or less the same place, was born from the works of **Plato**. It was called **Neo-Platonism** and its most important spokesman was a certain **Plotinus** (205–70 AD) who was born in Egypt, but had come to Rome to teach.

His theories were very much along the same lines as Philo's. Out of God (or 'the One' – as he called him) flow many *beings* or *emanations*, like water from a spring, or light from the sun (or toothpaste from a tube?). The further they got from the source, the dimmer they became until they just turned into darkness or matter (or dark matter) – having no real existence. Now between God (the source) and this matter, was the soul which acted on this matter and created the universe. This made matter the *substance* and soul the *form* (and if you believe this you'll bel...). Way out in the darkness, you'll be pleased to know, was the chilly matter that humans and animals are made of; but way, way out even further into dark, grey freezer-land, furthest from the light of God, were earth, water, stone and Tory politicians.

Jesus has been with us for a while now, and the early Christians were quick to get in on the 'What's It All About' act. These self-styled *Apologists* favoured a mish-mash of Greek philosophy and their own faith, pointing to a universe that didn't just consist of matter, but contained an eternal, unchanging and most of all, jolly good God. He is in everything, they claimed, and everything is in Him. He is both Plato's *ideas* and Aristotle's *forms*. He holds all the forms and patterns and creates everything out of nothing. What a guy!

One of the big thinkers at the time was a chap called **Augustine** (later to win a sainthood). He'd been loads of things before he discovered the *Neo-Platonists* (followers of Plato) and the *Apologists* (who said that faith was provable by reason) and then **Christ**. He went along with everything the *Apologists* thought and added his own little special thought that God had had all this universe business in his mind way back before time (or *Coronation Street*) began. In fact, if the truth be told, God created time and space to put the universe into.

But professional Christian thinkers went further than all that Greek form and matter chatter. They wouldn't take the old Greek idea that matter simply existed, and tried to get God in on the act. They said that He had to create some matter, so that He could have something to make all the stuff that goes to make up the universe, out of. His (God's) ideas, they all agreed, were simply divine. Basically, however, Augustine thought that philosophical reason could only go so far in religious affairs. Faith was what was required and, if you had it, God would tell you all you needed to know.

Augustine lived in the fourth century (354–450 AD to be precise), just in time to see the extremely rough and rather common barbarian hordes pouring south into the erstwhile Great Roman Empire, which was beginning to decline and fall. Time in fact to see the drawing of the curtains on the Roman and Greek civilizations and the official blowing out of the light, ready for the Dark Ages.

CHAPTER 3

The Extremely Dark Ages

After Augustine, nobody gave thinking about the universe a thought (unless you lived somewhere so remote that nobody gave a monkey's what you thought). Actually the Arabs had their sticky hands on most of the philosophical gear by now, as they'd overrun Alexandria where all the books were. And didn't they do well!

But in Europe, if asked, the non-'thinkers' would simply trot out the half-remembered stuff that Aristotle, Plato and all the other old Greeks had written. They were as happy as pigs in .... er ... mire, grovelling around for nigh-on seven hundred years telling grim(m) folk tales and singing naff folk songs about Pied Pipers and Robin Hoods to each other (*hey-nonny-no* and all that stuff) while cruise(ade)ing up the Holy Land whenever possible.

Then, in the ninth century, when the Christian religion had a stronghold on western Europe, a few chaps got together and started 'thinking' again. Actually, they thought, but didn't talk (unless these thoughts fitted exactly with Christian beliefs – or unless they weren't that

29

bothered about parting company with their heads!).

The chaps that did do the talking (and only as long as God was included) were known as **Scholastics** and they were around from the ninth to the thirteenth centuries. The first of them was an Irish theologian **John Scotus Eriugena** (*c*.810–*c*.877), known oddly as John the Scot. He was a strange and enigmatic figure by all accounts but had certainly done his homework as far as the Greek philosophers were concerned. John did most of his work on the continent, particularly in the court of Charles the Bald (see follically challenged kings), where he got into loads of arguments about 'free will', particularly with a monk called **Gottschalk**.

Eriugena maintained that man is able to do things according to his own will, while the miffed monk reckoned (along with most others) that our actions and what happens to us are predetermined.

> There once was a man who said 'Damn!
> It is borne in upon me I am
> An engine that moves
> In predestinate grooves;
> I'm not even a bus, I'm a tram.'
>
> M. E. HARE

Also, John suggested, since God is *one* and not divided, the universe must be a unity (Universe United). OK, everything *looks* different, but when you get down to it, everything is one (including man), and *all* God. Therefore the universe is simply an expression of the thought of God. This was (and is) called **Pantheism**.

Pierre Abelard (1079–1142) was a very famous French philosopher, famous almost as much for his chaotic, and somewhat tragic, lifestyle as for the writings he left. (Details can be read in his jolly book *Historia Calamitatum Mearum – The Story of My Misfortunes.*) And boy, did poor Pierre have misfortunes. For a start he fell in love with and wanted to marry one of his students, a young Parisian chick called Héloïse, whose uncle was a rather unpleasant canon called Fulbert. In 1118 Fulbert decided to sever their relationship by getting his sons to sever poor Abelard's vital marriage equipment one dark night. Abelard got the message and retired, somewhat lighter, to a monastery where he dedicated himself to work. (Héloïse got herself to a nunnery seeing there wasn't much point hanging around Abelard any more.) Abelard had always been vain, argumentative and big-headed, but after the event his critics (the other monks) added *angry* to the list (and who can blame him?).

His philosophy went like this. Discussion using logic or persuasion is the only way to get to truth – apart from the Scriptures. Even though the Empiricists (who were waiting to be invented – see chapter 6) wouldn't have it, this idea opened up a lot of healthy argument in smoke-(incense)-filled monasteries. In his book *Know Thyself*, which was all about ethics, he held out that sin can be defined as wilfully rejecting the wishes of God; action being less important than, say, the state of mind one's in when one does whatever it is one's doing. Continuing this argument, he maintained that when

31

Jesus gave his life for us – the 'atonement' – it was simply done as a brilliant gesture and example for us poor, sinful mortals to follow.

Abelard lived at a time when thinkers were beginning to question the overbearing dominance of the church, especially when the 'proofs' offered were so dodgy (even though Abelard thought they weren't), and a time when education was also slipping away from the church in favour of burgher (not McDonald's) or guild schools. Although poor Abelard was convinced that human reason could prove the Christian doctrines to be true, he failed to realize that merely allowing them to be questioned, weakened their stability. In other words, 'if it ain't broke, don't fix it'. Once this process of questioning started, however, nothing would stop the ball rolling.

Meanwhile, over on the other side of the world, the Arabs were now making themselves heard loud and clear. Creeping into southern Europe, they educated the natives with all the wise words of Aristotle, Plato and Co. that those 'Middle-Aged' silly-billies had forgotten. The trouble was that, as I mentioned in the last bit, the Europeans were only just beginning to wrestle with 'The Big Problem'. Who should they believe – the Ancient Greeks or God?

Although he sounds rather ordinary name-wise, **Roger Bacon** (*c.*1214–92) was far from that. He was an English Franciscan monk and part-time philosopher and scientist known to all as 'Doctor Mirabilis' ('marvellous doctor'). Bacon had got his hands on the only recently de-X-rated, and highly forbidden works of Aristotle, and the stuff he wrote himself was a heady concoction of Aristotle, other Greek and Arabic science, astrology and studies of the supernatural. His great work, which he titled rather cockily, *Opus Maius* ('Great Work') listed all the things that had tripped up the natural course of philosophy in the past.

Bacon's work is now reckoned to have remarkable foresight (though a bit patchy in overall quality), especially in maths, the science of optics (he invented specs, don't you know?) and because of the importance he gave to the correct use of experience and language. Unlike his Franciscan chum **Bonaventura**, who saw the 'new' science as an interesting field for investigation (but one which would eventually get in the way of praying), Bacon saw a fab new method which, by applying mathematical and philosophical techniques to the study of both philosophy and theology, would transform man's approach to learning. His monky mates, however, were less than thrilled with his work and poor Rog was condemned for 'suspected novelties'. Exactly how suspect these 'novelties' were we'll probably never know, but it's worth mentioning that they were certainly enough to put him behind bars for a while.

Around this time, there was another philosopher-cum-theologian, called **Thomas Aquinas** (1225–74), from a little village between Rome and Naples called (coincidentally?) Aquino, who put the God into Aristotle, so to speak. Aquinas wanted to show that the universe was reasonable and that universal *truths* (see below 1–3) were real. These 'universals', he thought, lived in everything and made them exactly what they were. They could be reached both through Christian faith (the easy, quick way) or through reason and the senses (the not-so-easy, slow way). He also reckoned he could prove the actual existence of God through the teachings of Aristotle, which was a bit cheeky, seeing as Aristotle hadn't even heard of our 'God'.

········ THE TRUTHS ········

1. What's (the) Matter?
Take an apple tree again. The *real* thing about an apple tree is not its leaves, bark, twigs or even its apples. These are simply the features that make it different from other trees. What makes this particular tree a tree, is its very *treeness* which is universal (and present in every other kind of tree). So it is the *matter* that makes an apple tree different from any other tree and it is the amount of matter in each different type of tree that makes them so different. This premise (or truth) can be applied to the whole universe, which then becomes simply a series of combinations of matter and universals. Geddit?

2. God, according to Thomas (later sainted for his lifetime contribution to truth), made the world from absolutely nothing, and can still be observed creating it every time he brings out a new product (babies, apples, *My Little Pony* etc).

3. Despite all this excessive wonderfulness, I'm afraid to report that Saint Tom followed Aristotle down the extremely politically incorrect 'woman-is-an-incomplete-man' path. He

believed that everything was a progression: from plants – to animals – to humans – to angels – to God himself. Unfortunately poor *woman* landed up somewhere between animal and man (don't blame me!). Luckily, in Heaven, he said (hedging his bets), there was total equality, on account of angels being sexless and having no gender (or presumably anything else!).

CHAPTER 4

. . . .

Off We Go Again : The Renaissance

All was not well with the relationship between religion and philosophy as we head towards the Renaissance that began in Northern Italy in the late fourteenth century. Philosophy and science were having a secretive affair, and religion, or should I say theology, was feeling a touch left out as it became more and more difficult to connect God with the formation of the universe. Not to be outdone, theology flirted with reason but most thinking people realized that they couldn't reach God through reason alone (or Rationalism p.51) because, when you got right down to it God, like Superman, was, and always would be, unknowable.

On top of all this there was a strong wave of what came to be known as **Individualism**. This was the realization that as well as being human beings, men (and women) were unique individuals. This opened the way for a complete no-holds-barred worship of genius. The ideal Renaissance man, therefore, would be one of universal genius, capable of understanding all aspects of science, art and indeed life. Unfortunately, the change was all a bit quick, which meant that many of the philosophers around this time were caught somewhere between the future and the past . . .

Nicholas de Cusa (1401–64), was a German cardinal and Bishop of Brixen. He still thought that the universe was God broken into little bits, but that in each little bit God was complete. As he believed that God was unknowable, he therefore reckoned that *all* human knowledge was just learned ignorance, which I think sounds a bit cocky, Nick.

Ludovico Vives (1492–1540), a sixteenth-century Spaniard, trashed everything that had been written in the past about the world (or God for that matter). He said that all his philosopher mates should go out into the fields and study nature. He also said that there was too much arguing about the nature of things and not enough real experimentation to find out how nature actually worked (see Darwin). That way, and that way only, he claimed, would we ever get control of it. In a way, although dabbling in magic and mystery, Vives and his contemporaries were beginning, almost accidentally, to show the way towards pure, proper, modern science.

The trouble was that scientific equipment was a bit iffy to say the least, so philosophers and scientists were having to turn to magic more and more. If only they had the right word (*abracadabra?*) or the right spell (*eye of newt, wart of toad?*). The resulting, new-fangled *Alchemy* was a semi-scientific, semi-hocus-pocus solution. Everyone from Leonardo da Vinci to our own Isaac Newton dabbled with experiments to find not only the elixir of life but, even better, a way of turning ordinary metals into gold (which sure would have revolutionized the scrap-metal business!).

The Swiss alchemist **Theophrastus Bombastus von Hohenheim** (1493–1541) (**Paracelsus** for short) thought and taught that man had two bodies and one soul. The body that one walked around with, made love with or hit other people with, came from the earth, and the other body (the invisible one) came from the stars. The soul, as you might have guessed, came from God. The three basic substances that everything was made of – sal (all solids), mercury (all liquids) and sulphur (all that caught fire) – were ruled by the spirits. As all nature was the home of strange spirits, he thought the only way to control it was with magic spells and magic words. This, as you can imagine, seems like a retrograde step, but when you think back to what had gone on in the Dark Ages, it wasn't that surprising. Gradually, however, all this superstitious nonsense began to sound simply too ridiculous and a few smart guys came along who harked back to a time when men used their common sense. More and more free thinkers made themselves available to revel in the reawakening of the world – the Renaissance.

By far the most important of these was an Italian chap called **Galileo Galilei** (1564–1642), who still liked the sound of old Democritus' atomic theories (see p.9). With the help of his brand-new, dead-powerful telescope (and his new chum, Keppler), he was able to back up Copernicus' theory that the earth revolved around the sun and not vice versa. He had to keep it under his voluminous beard, as the stuffy church didn't like it one bit – especially when our boy Isaac Newton went on to prove this conclusively. But why should this revelation upset the church and, anyway, what had this got to do with philosophy? Galileo, you see, was first and foremost a scientist – one of the first. For him, the discovery of the universe was simply a matter of science and mathematics. God, and all that, was for church, and priests, he said, should concentrate on the soul and not the stratosphere. At last it looked possible that at some time in the near future religion and philosophy could go their separate ways. But not for long.

Galileo was also important for his *Laws of Inertia*, which, although not exactly philosophy, is interesting anyway. He stated that things remain in the state that they are in, when either still or moving, as long as nothing comes along to change the situation. In simple language: if Galileo had dropped his ice cream whilst driving his Ferrari (neither of which he had) travelling at 120 mph, would it have dropped in his lap instead of flying over his shoulder and splatting against the rear window? Answer ... Yes! This is because the ice cream was enjoying the ride as much as he was, and was travelling through space at the same speed as his motor. If he'd been riding a motor-scooter it would have been a different matter.

Before we get into proper philosophy again it might be worth looking at the writings of **Niccolo Machiavelli** (1469–1527) as a reward for having lasted the course thus far. His ambition was to create a united Italian nation and at the same time show the church exactly what he thought of them. He suggested that if you have a country riddled with sleazy corruption (sound familiar?) the best way to rule it is by appointing a complete and utter, fully paid-up, no-holds-barred, meanie. OK, freedom would be the loser at first, but Machiavelli thought this would be a necessary stage for his fellow man to go through on his way to becoming less corrupt (dodgy or what?). Anyway, to achieve this, the ruler (a prince in this case) should be free to use any device, be it force, deceit, or breaking of the law, as a means to fight trickery with trickery and corruption with corruption. Whether one agrees or not, many modern societies have obviously taken handfuls of leaves out of old Machiavelli's books (see Watergate, Irangate or even Margate).

Time for a little more bacon. **Francis Bacon** (1561–1626), a Londoner, followed Galileo by saying that, as nothing in religion could actually be proved, there was little point wasting breath talking about it. This made him (along with Galileo) one of the first of a long line of great **Empiricist** philosophers (who believed that all knowledge should be based on observation, experience and experiment). He thought religion was unimportant compared to science and to try to delve into it was like courting a virgin dedicated to God … barren and capable of producing nothing (his words not mine! And dead dangerous words, especially in those days!). Everything in the universe, according to our Francis, acted according to strict laws, which, when fully understood, would explain everything. Bacon never got around to constructing his own theory of the universe, but it was said of him that his efforts amounted to a working map of what lay ahead for men to learn. He was a sort of prophet looking over a promised land of scientific knowledge.

Mr Bacon died of pneumonia trying to freeze a chicken in a snow drift on Hampstead Heath (don't even ask). Perhaps he should have started with peas (or bacon).

Thomas Hobbes (1588–1679), another Empiricist Englishman, would have nothing to do with all that dusty old Greek philosophy and precious little to do with God (hence his nickname 'The Beast of Malmesbury') and concerned himself with material things. He did, however, credit God with kick-starting the whole caboodle. Everything in our universe, he said, is in perpetual motion, set off admittedly by Him at the creation (suspiciously like the Big Bang theory). As all these bodies whizz around, they influence each other, creating or destroying 'accidents'. These accidents, as he called them, exhibit the characteristics of the various bodies, such as motion, rest, colour and hardness. Motion is the continuous giving up of one space by a body and the assuming of another – a bit like cosmic musical chairs.

Say you are asleep on the sofa. Thomas Hobbes would have called this an accident of rest. Now say your pet Rottweiler waltzes up and bites you firmly upon the bum. Hobbes would have said that the second body (your doggie) had destroyed your accident of rest and created an accident of motion (you're not kidding, Tommy!). This is what he called the law of 'cause and effect'. As one accident 'dies', another is created. Apply this to everything in the universe, and you might understand what he was going on about (or you might not).

Hobbes was one of the first philosophers

to relate his philosophy to the savage world around him. He recognized that the universal need and desire for self-preservation gave rise to a basic right for man to use any means open to him. In fact, he believed that man has the right to do *anything* he blinking well wants. But if one realizes that this is indeed man's nature, then try imagining a society without any social or civil order ... It doesn't take a brainiac, said Hobbes, to see the need for an order to emerge as a way of preventing everyone declaring war on each other. The answer to all this, said our Tom, is to appoint an all-powerful king or queen, or at least some sort of assembly or government. OK, the individual might lose his freedom but it sure beats having your head knocked off. Even if the ruler turns out to be a really nasty bit of work, throwing his weight around all the time, it has to be better than the bloody mess his subjects would get themselves into if he wasn't there (and that, dear reader, sounds like pure Machiavelli: p.40).

> Thomas Hobbes of Malmesbury thought
> Life was 'nasty and brutish and short';
> But contracts once made,
> Would come to our aid
> And ensure modest comfort – at court.
> PETER ALEXANDER

. . . .

CHAPTER 5

Philosophy Goes Modern

A jolly clever Frenchman, **René Descartes** (1596–1650), is generally recognized to be the father of modern philosophy. He was known as a bit of a doubter and because he doubted absolutely everything (even his own body sometimes), his theory of knowledge began with what he called a 'quest for certainty' (a definite starting point or foundation on which to build). His famous *'I think, therefore I am'* quip features in the top ten of all-time clever things to say. It meant (as if you didn't know) that by being able to doubt things he at least *must* be thinking (he thought). If he could only do that *one* thing, it followed that he must be a 'thinking being' and could therefore be trusted to exist far more than any of the things around him that could only be experienced through his senses. One is tempted to wonder what Madame Descartes thought of this?

There was a young student called Fred
Who when questioned on Descartes said:
'It's perfectly clear
That I'm not really here,
For I haven't a thought in my head'.

V. R. ORMOROD

He threw all that stuff about forms, ideas or universals out of the window, like a mental car boot sale. He preferred to start from scratch with the simplest idea, before rolling on to more complex problems — just like we do in life. Nature, he claimed, must be explained mechanically. At the bottom of everything, from a sugar cube to a star, is *substance*, and this substance doesn't need anything else to exist. Substance comes in two forms, *mind* and *body* which, although capable of getting along perfectly well without each other, both depend on that great big substance in the sky — you guessed it — God. God, he claimed, was like a concept tattooed on the 'remembering' bit of our brains at birth.

Thought (or *mind*), whether a big thought or a little thought, said Descartes, takes up no room in space and therefore can't be subdivided. *Body*, on the other hand, has length, breadth and thickness (particularly mine!) called 'extension', as can be observed in all the different things floating around in the universe, which are all the different types of *substance*.

Even further, he went on, there are no spaces or voids in the universe. Bodies fill all spaces (as can be observed in the London Underground at rush-hour), and these can be chopped up into smaller and smaller bits *ad infinitum*. Since there is no such thing as empty space, motion is not just a question of things shifting around occupying recently vacated places (like musical chairs again), but should be thought of more like the flow of liquids. *Extension* (length, breadth and thickness), therefore, can be divided into any number of weeny particles that can regroup, should they so desire, into different forms of matter.

········· I BARK, THEREFORE I'M NOT? ·········

Descartes was obviously not big on pets. As the poor things couldn't actually think, he claimed, they were basically no more than automatons or robots (sorry, Rover). He should have seen some movies with stars like *Lassie*. That clever mutt could do practically everything from first aid to advanced computer programming. As for Flipper the dolphin ... Man, on the other hand, both thinks and takes up space in space (some more than others) which makes him a *dual* creature (and makes Descartes a **Dualist**).

Descartes fell ill with pneumonia in 1649 during a brief teaching stint at the Court of Queen Christina. On his death bed he was heard to mutter *Ça, mon âme, il faut partir* ('So, my soul, it is time to depart'): that's Dualism for you! The poor guy blamed arch-feminist Christina for his imminent death as he claimed she made him get up too early (I know the feeling) to work. It's more likely, however, that he died from catching cold, as the philosopher Grotius had done when visiting her draughty court six years earlier.

Benedict de Spinoza (1632–77), a Dutch-Jewish philosopher, didn't go a bundle on this dualist business, and taught that there was only one 'substance' and this substance was – here we go again – God. All the bits and pieces in the universe are actually one big whole (as opposed to hole). This made him a **Monist**.

Imagine a huge brick wall, with graffiti on either side. One side has one design on it but if we look at the other we get a completely different picture. Spinoza said that it was the same with substance: look at it from one position and it's *body*; seen from the other side it's *mind*. He called one *extension*, the other *mind*. Everything in the universe, be it water, stone, wind, animal, man (and even the insurance salesman) is a part of God, and every object is also both extension (body) and mind. You can't have mind without body or vice versa. This also made him a **Pantheist** (a *monist-pantheist?*).

Man, he claimed, is just another a form of God or the universal substance. Each individual (including you) is a copy, or mode, of body and thought. In all the other non-human things these two modes of body and thought are fairly straight forward (trust us to be different) but we humans are far more complex (Benny Hill? Surely not) and are composed of many parts. On top of that, in man, mind is conscious of its own actions (kinda self-conscious?).

Having said this, man's mind and body don't really have much to do with each other and neither will do what the other tells it to. As they both tend to knock around together, however, what happens to one tends to happen to the other. That's why our minds *seem* to be affected by what happens to our bodies (this sounds like the beginnings of a lecture on the evils of drink).

To sum up the world according to Spinoza (if I dare): all the universe is God or substance, in the form of both mind and body. Man is simply one unit in the whole sorry business. He is, when it comes right down to it, simply mind and body (phew!!!), though he can never have free will or a free soul, as these poor things will always be trapped within his mechanical body.

Spinoza got himself into huge trouble (if you call excommunication and nearly being assassinated, trouble) with the Jewish overlords when he claimed that you could take most of the Bible with a pinch of salt as it only really applied to the time it was written. Our Jesus was still his main man, however, as He (Jesus) preached a 'religion of reason' which put love at the top of the heap. Spinoza was cast out of Amsterdam (no bad thing) but crept back and earned a living polishing lenses (until the glass dust killed him), whispering his thoughts only to selected audiences.

CHAPTER 6

. . . .

Empiricists and All That

Like most other seventeenth-century philosophers, Descartes and Spinoza were **Rationalists**, as they both believed in the importance of reason as the primary source of all knowledge, and that human beings have certain ideas and concepts implanted in their minds when a mere twinkle in their father's eye. This idea had come right through from Plato and Socrates and had hung around throughout the Middle Ages.

The seventeenth century, however, spawned a new batch of philosophers who thought that was all a bunch of clap-trap. These chaps thought, when it came right down to it, that our minds are a blank canvas at birth and whatever we end up with we've put there ourselves. This might not seem like a big deal to you, but in a Rationalist world dominated by tradition and superstition, it was quite radical, if not rather outrageous. They were called **Empiricists** and their hero was Aristotle.

John Locke (1632–1704) was probably our very best, home-grown philosopher (along with Russell – see p.114). He came from an aristocratic background and was loaded (very useful if you're going to spend your life just thinking). His patron was the Earl of Shaftesbury, who was eternally grateful (wallet-wise) when Locke (also a doc) supervised a major operation to remove something very unpleasant from his liver, leaving him with a little silver (and large financial) drainage tap for the rest of his life.

I digress. John Locke, although an empiricist, actually quite liked old Descartes and even went to France to study his work. When push came to shove, however, he thought the not-long-dead philosopher was on a dodgy wicket. Locke reckoned that all human understanding was based on experience, sensation and then reflection. But is there a real world really out there to reflect upon, he asked, or are we imagining it? Locke said there was. (Thank heavens for that, or there'd be no point writing this book – or anything else for that matter.) It is our senses, he went on, that tell us about this world. Let's face it, we run around experiencing all its wonders (and disasters) every day so, of course, we *can* say it exists … We might not know much about the cause of our sensations but, as shop assistants always seem to say, 'that's another department'. The mere fact that sensations are caused, proves there's a real world to cause 'em. He didn't go right to the end of the long and lonesome Empiricist trail, however, as he said that the 'ability' to know things comes from God (who knows it all anyway). But, he said, all this is only probable. There are no certainties.

Although seen as 'the man in the boiler room' by top natural scientists, Boyle (of law fame) and Newton, Locke confessed that he was extremely doubtful about whether you could actually call what they did 'proper science' as they could never, in a million years, give us that God-like peek into the real essence of things.

Locke agreed with his fellow Empiricists that we humanoids come into the world stupid, or should I say brain-clean, but at least have the power to receive whatever sensory information is thrown at us. (Actually, I've known a lot of people who leave the world not much better, but we won't go into that now.) He was, therefore, big on education, seeing it as a) the process of learning through experience with the outside world, and b) the toiling towards a realization of happiness (and so say all of us!). His ideal was a sound mind neatly zipped into a sound body. If this sounds like it's getting perilously close to the publicity for a Christian Science gymnasium, you're absolutely right. Locke thought you should throw everything (educationally – that is) at kids and that they should be fit enough to take it. A perfect human should be able to communicate with everyone, should be able to take care of himself at all times and have enough know-how to meet the demands of his environment (just like Arnie Schwarzenegger?).

One of his books gave an account of a large cross-section of current ideas, dividing them into 'simple' and 'complex'. Nice simple ideas, such as red, cold and bitter, are all they appear to be, having no other little ideas within them. These, like atoms, can neither be made nor destroyed by us. Put a few of these simple ideas together, and you get a complex idea, according to Locke. We humans, he went on, are quite capable of mixing up simple ideas thereby creating complex ones that have never existed before – like the unicorn or any of those half-horse half-man half-goat half-bird (and half-wit) weirdos that buzzed around Greece in ancient times.

He also went on about primary and secondary qualities, as had his old idol Descartes. 'Primary qualities' were things like size, heaviness, motion, number and so on. If we throw a bunch of bananas across a room, for instance, all of the above qualities can be sensed objectively. We can then ascribe the bananas further qualities like colour, smell, taste, hotness or coldness (ever taken a banana's temperature?). These, however, are not real qualities as they reproduce only the effect of the outer reality on our senses. Those first qualities are the same whichever bunch of bananas you chucked, but the second qualities will vary from banana to banana, person to person and even (we presume) animal to animal. The smell that you call a 'bananary' smell might be a totally different 'bananary' smell to someone else's.

When applying this line of thought to ethics, however, Locke believed that certain principles applied to everyone, and that they were man's *natural right* (the only Rationalistic bit of his thoughts). This, as you might have guessed, applied to a belief in – yes – God. He believed it was inherent in human reason (not just faith) to be able to *know* that God exists.

George Berkeley (1685–1753), was an Irish bishop who had quite a few problems with Locke's philosophy that all we can *know* are our ideas, and also with his assumption that there was a world out there that causes our sensations. George therefore asked the following question: if the basis of knowledge is sensation, and reflection upon sensation, how the hell can we ever *know* that a world of bodies, or things, as distinct from our *ideas* of bodies (or things) actually exists? Berkeley realized that Locke was batting on a dodgy wicket as he could not possibly prove the existence of this world on the basis of his philosophy. And further still, being a passionate believer in God he figured that the only way to trash atheism (nonbelief in God) once and for all, was to disprove belief in matter (or stuff, or substance, or body). Forget all that universe-of-material-objects mumbo-jumbo. All we can prove is that we *have* ideas (hold on, haven't we been round this block before?).

Do we create ideas ourselves? Of course not. They come from God. Let's face it, said Berkeley, God must be bright enough to suss that there's no need to create material objects which would cause ideas in us; it's much simpler for Him to bypass the middle man and simply cause the ideas we have without bothering with matter. We might not know exactly who or what He is, but we do know the results of all His hard graft ... IDEAS! Berkeley, like Locke, believed that nothing in the universe was really there unless it was observed and understood. That's funny, I don't understand my mother-in-law (ex), but I'm absolutely sure she's there . . .

Look at it this way. I'm sitting in a room with a couple of pals watching *Blind Date* (sad life or what?). I look around me and see the empty beer cans, the bookcase, the three-piece Laura Ashley-covered suite (only kidding) etc. Berkeley would have asked if they were actually real, as for him all the things around him were simply ideas and not material objects (that's Irish for you).

Back to the sitting room and *Blind Date*. I suddenly need the toilet. When I leave the room, do the objects disappear? Do they come to the lavatory with me in my mind? (Cilla Black in the loo ... No thanks!) Do they exist in any-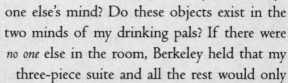one else's mind? Do these objects exist in the two minds of my drinking pals? If there were *no one* else in the room, Berkeley held that my three-piece suite and all the rest would only have existed in the mind of God (He's welcome). All the time, however, they are not material objects – according to Berkeley – they're simply ideas.

So basically Berkeley debunked a material universe. If objects weren't in his mind, my mind (or your mind) they must be in God's mind. They might *seem* to be material but they're not, and that's the end of it. Hold fast, I've just got to get the idea of my bike out and ride it down to the idea of my doctor's surgery – my brain (or the idea of my brain) hurts!

The philosopher Berkeley once said
In the dark to a maid in his bed:
'No perception, my dear,
Means I'm not really here,
But only a thought in your head.'
P. W. R. FOOT

The most important of the British Empiricists was a Scot called **David Hume** (1711–76). He also high-tailed it off to France at an early age, to get closer to where the big boys in philosophy (like Descartes) had lived and studied. Later in life he ended up as England's chargé d'affaires in Paris and nearly married a rich Countess, but failed owing to her 'affairs' with an even richer prince (or a man formerly known as a prince). Hume was once described, when a little older, as resembling a 'fat, well-fed Benedictine Monk'. But I'm getting off the track.

In his *Treatise of Human Nature*, David Hume showed that natural science was all he was really concerned with – that and bringing real experimental method into the study of the human mind. He searched for some order in what appeared to be chaos in natural systems. You might be relieved to know that, for once, God had nothing to do with it, as Dave could find no good reason for his existence. But he did agree with Berkeley that things only exist if you could actually perceive them. He even went a bit further and said that when one left a room the objects in it no longer existed (bang goes my telly). For Hume nothing of substance existed. All we have, he said, is a continuous flow of ideas piling up on each other. When we go for a walk, for instance, the notions come thick and fast: front door – path – pavement – bus stop – passengers – conductor – no money – pavement again. Thus, he went on, there's no evidence of God – or nature, come to that.

Hume saw himself as a sort of cleaner-upper of all the piles of old ideas and daft unthought-out concepts from the

Middle Ages onwards. He was like a chap that goes round emptying waste-paper baskets in an office full of indecisive people and comes back in the morning with everything sorted out neatly. He would never believe in things that he couldn't actually witness. Therefore, miracles, ghosts, spirits, angels, pixies, Father Christmas and Kylie Minogue were not even to be considered. All he could be sure of was this stream of ideas. Where did the ideas come from? Nobody knows. What was their purpose? Nobody knows. Where are they are actually going? Nobody knows. In fact, thinking men all came to the same conclusion: if you follow David Hume – where do you get to? All together now ... NOBODY KNOWS!

Hume was the most important and over-the-top of the Empiricists and he took it to its logical conclusion. Namely, that reason is entirely subordinate to sense; that knowledge is only built on the senses and therefore that every single idea must be born out of sensation. So, for instance, the *idea* of cause and effect (that is, 'causality' as a concept or idea) must also be derived from sensation. Causality, therefore, can itself be observed. For example, say we drink ten pints of Old Gobbler and fall over, we can then see that, in most cases, one follows the other. The ten pints (or four in my case) are the *cause* of the falling over (which is the *effect*). Knowledge of causality, in any case you care to mention, can, as in the above example, only come from observation – which is not, therefore, knowledge of causality – it's simply prediction. This all leads to what Hume is most remembered for – **Scepticism** (see also Descartes p.45).

Cried the maid: 'You must marry me, Hume!'
A statement that made David fume,
He said: 'In cause and effect,
There is a defect;
That it's mine you can only assume.'

P. W. R. FOOT

You've gotta be pretty clever to go to university at fifteen and young **Gottfried Wilhelm Leibniz** (1646–1716) certainly was just that. After much study and presumably star-gazing from his bedroom window, he maintained that from where he was lying, the most important characteristic of all the bodies in the universe is force – or 'the tendency of the body to move or continue its motion' (sounds rather distasteful).

He worked out that each individual thing has a corresponding notion or idea known only to God, from which He (God) can deduce all the characteristics possessed by that said individual at any time throughout his (or her) life. Unlike Spinoza, who reckoned there was only one substance, Leibniz reckoned that there were an infinite number, all maintained by God. The world that all these substances go to make up is the best one possible, because that's the way it is – so there! Each substance is dead simple (without component bits), and he called each one a *monad* (unit). Plants and the like are rather vague wispy sorts of monads, slightly clearer ones go to make up animals, while we humans are clearer still (which is nice to know), but the clearest monad of all is God (as if you hadn't guessed).

Each mini-monad expresses the whole universe, and since

it has no doors or windows nothing can get in to influence it, so it remains the same from the very beginning of time. Living things contain a soul which rounds up and guides all the other monads, sheep dog-like, in the-thing-itself. Although monads don't have anything to do with each other, they all seem to get along pretty well (God willed it that way). When a monad decides to do something, the others don't pay attention, or pretend not to. But because of the way they were created, they tend to all the same. So when push comes to shove all those pesky monads work together in the same way as various parts of an organism. Whether you can get your head round all this or not, Leibniz (rather smugly, I think) reckoned that he'd tied everything in science to everything in Christianity (Holy Monads). The universe was basically scientific, but when it came right down to it, God ruled – OK.

CHAPTER 7

. . . .

The Age of Enlightenment

It would be fair to say that although the centre of European thinking had been England at the beginning of the eighteenth century, the focus swung to France around the middle and then towards Germany towards the end. The French thinkers were labelled **Enlightenment Philosophers** and many had visited England where, despite having to suffer the terrible grub, they felt freer to express themselves. The three stars were Montesquieu, Voltaire and Rousseau who all based their thinking on our boy Locke, liking his ideals of toleration, freedom and government by constitution. They also echoed old Socrates and the Stoics (see p.11 and p.22) with a total faith in reason above all else, dedicating themselves to laying a foundation for morals, religion and ethics that applied to everyday living.

With a name like **Charles Louis de Secondat, baron de Montesquieu** (1689–1755) you can bet he'd been born very much on the right side of *les tracks*. The aristocracy were being given a bit of a hard time by the monarchy at this period of France's history, so it's not really surprising that not only did he spend time laying the aforementioned foundations, but also much richer women (in an effort to climb socially and pursue his often ill-hidden greed). He will be remembered for his theory of the separation of powers: that is, the shoving of all legislative, executive and judicial powers on to independent bodies. Strangely enough, they liked the sound of this in America and so Montesquieu had a great influence on the Founding Fathers.

It was all very well being enlightened yourself, but the French enlightenment philosophers soon sussed that if the movement was to stand any chance at all, they must educate the filthy masses and the only way to do that was through their even filthier children. This way, and this way only, would mankind make any progress, though once they had established this premise they turned about face (see great philosophical pastimes) and started querying the whole point of civilizing the multitude.

Jean Jacques Rousseau (1712–78), the French writer, spent his whole life restlessly shifting from country to country, job to job and faith to faith (and mistress to mistress), most of the time not feeling very well (serves him right!).

He had shot his mouth off about the merits of the 'general will of the people' rather than the 'social contract in politics'. He blurted this out twenty-seven years before the revolution and supported the idea of the individual being voluntarily 'kept down' in favour of the general collective will, on the patronizing basis that, though one might not like it, it was for one's own good. Rousseau rather smartly called it being 'forced to be free'. This, of course, appeals to all those clever so-and-so's who see themselves as prime movers in a party that know, and are determined to enforce, the supreme collective will – 'for the good of all'. (Like the late, 'great' Margaret Thatcher?)

He also thought that the arts and sciences were rubbish, or in his words, contributed nothing to the virtue or happiness of the human being, but instead brought ruin and corruption. This was odd for a man who spent a large amount of his time writing naff operas and dirty plays. He also said that society messes up the child and that its influence is wholly evil (like le video game and le breakfast telly), so much so that one should protect the nipper until he is so together that society cannot destroy his inner nature. I say *he*, because Rousseau didn't seem to care to much about girls and didn't think anyone should bother to train them. They should be educated, he said, to serve men and make them happy. They should be fitted into a pattern demanded of men while men should be free to develop according to their own inner nature. I reckon that if he'd written that sort of rubbish these days, he'd be in the same boat as Salman Rushdie. He should be remembered as the first true philosopher of **Romanticism** (see next chapter).

A hopeful old fellow called Rousseau
Saw that man was not born bad, but grew so;
If you change his surrounding,
You'll find grace abounding –
You must turn the clock back to do so.

JOHN FAY

François Marie Arouet de Voltaire (1694–1778) (no wonder he preferred plain Voltaire) was the last of this merry bunch of Empiricists and his satirical writing had gotten him exiled to Holland and England. When he returned to Paris, shortly before leaving the planet altogether, he was hailed as 'the greatest French champion of the enlightenment, and his generation's most courageous spokesman for freedom and toleration'. Not bad for someone who'd spent a large part of his life banged up behind bars.

Philosophically Voltaire drank a heady cocktail of science and empiricism with a large splash of religious awe for good measure. He lashed out about the evil doings of the king (see sure-fire ways of losing your head) and the unfair, one-sided privileges of the nobility. He was a believer in God but thought that the clergy were appalling and the Christian religion worse. 'Those who can make you believe in absurdities can make you commit atrocities.' Deeply concerned with the improvement of the human condition, Voltaire's writings were not just to massage his own conscience, but a call for a pulling-out of the corporate finger in order to act.

Isn't it nice to find a philosopher with a half-normal name. Jonathan Edwards (1703–58), born in South Windsor, Connecticut, is now thought of as one of the most brilliant philosophic minds to ever come out of the States (next to Ronald McDonald). He was a fully paid up Calvinist (believer that everything we do is predestined) and, influenced by the likes of Locke, ended up writing from the same side of the fence as Berkeley and the Brits, that the world as we know it was no more than a series of impressions for which we had to thank that great benefactor in the sky ... God. In fact, he continued, if we are to have any good points at all they can only be attained through the free gift of God, as humanity itself cannot drag itself out of the mire it has dug itself into without His help. Saying things like this gave Edwards a star role in the 'Great Awakening', New England's religious revival of the mid-eighteenth century.

After Hume, however, the next philosopher to change the ways of thinking was a German, **Immanuel Kant** (1724–1804). Probably one of the most famous of all modern philosophers, he was the son of a saddler and lived all his life in the town of Königsberg. In his masterwork *The Critique of Pure Reason*, finished in 1781, he set out to 'assure to reason its lawful claims, and dismiss all groundless pretensions, not by despotic decrees, but in accordance with its own eternal and unalterable laws'.

Kant had claimed that Hume had roused him from his 'dogmatic slumbers'; for he'd done away with metaphysics (any enquiry into reality that goes beyond science) which Kant had previously been quite nifty at. Having said that, he was determined to patch it up and restore it to the lofty position it had held before the Hume trouncing.

Kant, like Berkeley, found philosophy essential when digging around the foundations of his Christian belief, and fought to restore man to his rightful position – Dominator of the Universe (sounds like a sci-fi movie). He was not only a jolly brilliant professor and expert on all the other philosophers that had gone before him but, on his afternoon off, set out down his own personal trail with the questions, 'What is knowledge, and how is it possible? What can we really know, and how can we know it?' After much to-ing and fro-ing, he came to the conclusion that we humans can only really trust our own experiences, which, again, is what the empiricists were going on about.

But he wouldn't go all the way with Hume and his mates in that this logically led to the conclusion that *all* knowledge is derived from experience. Instead of all our knowledge conforming to objects, as Hume had reckoned, perhaps objects conform to our knowledge. The *way* in which we understand and reflect upon objects might actually mould our experience. Kant thought that we can have certain *a priori* (built-in) concepts concerning the way we treat reason as a basis for our belief in knowledge. These don't come from experience, but cannot be divorced from their application to sense experience (hearing, seeing, tasting etc). Everything we see causes some sort of sensation, be it a tree, a worm or a double-decker bus. But we can't possibly hope to know what causes these sensations.

So, I hear you ask (or not), if we can't work out something as simple as what causes a worm, how can we possibly hope to know the universe, which must exist way beyond the capacity of our weeny brains? Fear not. All the sensations that flood into our minds, said Kant, are turned into ideas. Using Reason (or intelligence) we can form an Idea (or notion) of not only the world but also the universe which goes far beyond above experience and gives us transcendular principles (who, *me?*).

As we experience the world, he went on, we begin to suspect that the world had no real beginning, that everything seems to follow the basic laws of nature and that no one *thing* caused it to be, or for that matter, bothers to keep it going. According to Kant, we humans must see it that way, as there's no other way to experience it. Well, that's telling us! We can, however, build up a world of Idea (or notion), which has no beginning; in which matter can be divided as much as you like; in which there is freedom from the laws of nature; and in which there is someone or something who (or what) gets the whole shooting match together – that great caretaker in the sky – He who must be obeyed – God!

Given the choice, Kant reckoned man should carry on as if this second world existed, if only to preserve his moral goodness. In fact, he said, this goodness is only *possible* if we act (or pretend?) as if this world exists, as it pushes us forward to reach our goals. If man lives in this world, therefore, he will be (even *has* to be) good – and we all want to be good, don't we? As for God, Kant thought He was the best idea a man could have (since Woman), and that his existence was essential for a moral life. There must be a God, he maintained, who is wise and good, to make a connection between goodness and happiness (and presumably to make sure we don't have too much of it!), and who knows everything, has absolute power and is in charge of our moral ideals (eat your heart out, Mary Whitehouse).

So this meant that for Kant there were two different worlds or universes. One of Experience (scientific) and one of Practical Reason. In his 'practical' world, Kant thought that man should work on one basic rule: 'Always act so that you can will the maxim of determining principle of your action to become universal law; act so you can will that everybody shall follow the principle of your actions.' Which, extremely crudely translated, means keep yourself under such control that if what you do becomes what everyone else does it wouldn't be so bad a thing (and always wear clean pants when crossing a busy road!). Follow this and it will give you (or mankind) the freedom and dignity that Hume (he thought) had almost destroyed. Kant finally argued that there is a truth way above anything a human could realize. Where? I hear you demand. This moral law is deep inside us and guarantees a world of worth or value.

Now all this was hopefully straightforward, but how, wondered Kant, does man find out the difference between right and wrong, or good and bad? Like Rousseau, he accepted that the only really 'Good Thing' was human self-control (or will) heavily 'breathed on' by a respect for moral law or duty, which means you won't get any brownie points for a moral act designed to make a fast buck, or done purely out of sympathy.

Therefore, providing you do things for the best of reasons (respecting that old moral law), you shouldn't lose too much sleep over the consequences. The moral law, he stated, is a part of reason itself, or *a priori* in the way we think. An *a priori* truth is one that can exist independently of observable or experimentable-on facts. Following on, if everything you do, you would be happy for anyone else to do (to you), then you can assume this is right. In other words 'do as you would be done by'. This could obviously be a dodgy premise in some circs. If, for instance, you had a predilection for wacky sexual practices (not me, I hasten to add), I dare say you wouldn't mind if everyone else had too. But would that make it right? (Answers on a postcard.)

Now Kant reckoned this law was installed in all of us, otherwise life on earth for us humanoids would be nigh on impossible. If we attempt to do the opposite, human get-togethers on any scale would be pure mayhem (but quite fun?). He wanted each individual, therefore, to act as if they ruled the whole universe, so that his or her own personal way of carrying on would automatically become the code of conduct of his people.

Unlike the world of nature — which stumbles around suffering the results of cause and effect (like eating each other) — man has to believe he has free will. The very existence of his moral conscience proves that he must have a choice in his actions. And if that ain't free will, what is?

All the philosophers that ever thought (or thought before Kant thought) had attempted to work out how we (the individuals), while living in our little world, and even littler environments, could actually *think*. Some had reckoned we simply faced the world like a blank message pad and received our ideas through the senses. Others didn't like that version and thought (as we've heard before) that we already had ideas as standard equipment and needed only a little gentle massage to bring them into consciousness.

Kant tried to drive a middle path (or even a different

path altogether), by suggesting that we *do* receive all the necessary gubbins from the environment, but that the mind is constructed so that it can shape them into ideas – just like a jelly in a mould. The mind was in fact one highly complex jelly mould (mine particularly) with bits sticking out and bits sticking in. As all the impressions pour in, they are shaped accordingly. Unlike real jelly moulds (cats, bunnies, piggies etc), all our minds are very similar, so therefore we think much the same as each other, and organize impressions in much the same way. But all these ideas are contained and shaped within our minds, so it doesn't follow that we can actually *know* the world outside our minds which he called *the-thing-in-itself* (watch this term). Sure we know it exists, and we can even run around adjusting our ideas as we take more into the jelly-mould, but that's all folks! That's as far as this train goes. Our ideas are made on the premises and are determined by the equipment we have at our disposal.

> The famous philosopher, Kant
> Said 'Why, when I run, do I pant?
> I fear t'would be treason
> To my Critique of Reason
> To think I'm unfit, so I shan't.'
>
> C. S. COOK

The names of **Johann Gottlieb Fichte** (1762–1814) and Kant go hand in hand, though on many basic things they disagreed. Johann was also German and was educated in theology and then philosophy at Jena University. His first book, which he didn't put his name to, was mistakenly attributed to Kant, which must have hacked Fichte off no end (and probably Kant). It was a combination of his almost challenging morality, his support for the French Revolution (always much safer when one's hundreds of miles away) and his constant thumbs-down to the known religions. It got Fichte into the sort of hot water that he seemed to luxuriate in. Continuing his favourite hobby of upsetting people, he tried his level best to break up student groups and then, just for good measure, stamped on the toes of the local clergy by lecturing on Sundays.

Fichte believed that the concept of God is the same as the concept of a world order based on morality, even if this in turn is the basis of how all knowledge is acquired and the only worthwhile objective way of viewing the real world. This implied, however, that there was no real reason to have God: this was practically atheism (belief that God doesn't exist) and really got up the noses of his contemporaries.

Working on Sundays, supporting revolutions, upsetting the students, even criticizing religions were all bad enough, but to question the actual point of God! That was going *too* far. It was the feather that broke the university's back, so his colleagues got together and fired him from his job at Jena.

Fichte was the very first to strip the transcendental or airy-fairy elements from the branch of philosophy that deals with the nitty-gritty of knowing and being, that Kant supported. Fichte maintained that realization (consciousness) was the only basis from which to explain our experiences. He did, however, join with Kant's conception of the moral life as an unattainable goal, so that all our existence becomes simply the unsatisfiable strivings of the bit of our mind that makes us individual (Ego). This, rambling on, puts forward the case that everything outside our minds got in the way of achieving this coveted righteous life.

....

CHAPTER 8

So Romantic

Romanticism was probably Europe's last great cultural shindig, and last joint peek under the sheets at contemporary thought. It began in Germany at the end of the eighteenth century and finally petered out in the middle of the nineteenth, having spread through Europe and even crept over to the States in the meantime. Everyone had had enough of the cool, stiff, rational logic of the 'Enlighteners' and all that horrid, stodgy, neo-classical art that went with it. They wanted to embrace the spontaneous, the subjective, the imaginative, the emotional and, most of all, the swashbucklingly heroic.

Philosophers didn't mind dabbling with Kant's 'free will' stuff, or the idea that reality is ultimately spiritual, or even his theory that nature is a mirror of the human soul, but they wanted passion and they wanted Art with a huge A; for it was Art and Art only, they cried, that could bring us closer to the inexpressible.

Composers like Beethoven took over from the Baroque chart-toppers Bach and Handel (who did it mostly for God), while poets like Wordsworth and Byron (who certainly didn't) wrote the rhymes. Whether you sat in the loo writing soppy poetry or tripped gaily through the fields studying the sex life of hosts of golden daffodils, it was all part of the same. Pursuits like mud-wrestling or darts would probably have been frowned upon and in the philosophy or the 'what-are-we-thinking-today' department, one man is remembered above all others.

Very much a 'Kant' man, **Friedrich Wilhelm Joseph von Schelling** (1775–1854) was a big influence on the English Romantics, particularly Coleridge. For Schelling, 'conscious-ness' itself was the only immediate object or point of all this knowledge business, as anything we knew of this world, out-side our heads, simply clogged up the method by which our thoughts and feelings became aware of themselves. Art alone, he claimed, allowed the mind to become fully aware of *itself* and all philosophical to-ing and fro-ing should be lurching towards that end (heaven help us!). Schelling also saw a kind of 'world spirit' in nature, and also in the human mind. The natural and the spiritual were therefore one and the same. He went on to claim that all the universe (including us lot) is One Big Thing. The individuals and even the tiny bits and pieces are all parts of this whole. Thus, for him, everything in nature was alive and kicking and wherever you look, you will find the spirit trying to fulfil its potential, whether it's in the trees, flowers, rocks or even in the sand castles. They are all the same as the human mind, but these last four are a bit 'unripe' or blind (three blind rocks?) compared to the fully realized consciousness of the human mind. Does this mean that rocks can't think as well as we do – but could if they tried harder? This slightly bizarre concept is also part of Pantheism (God is everything, everything is God, p.31).

Georg Wilhelm Hegel (1770–1831) was born in Stuttgart, Germany, and studied at Tübingen alongside chaps like Schelling, when the Romantic era was in full swing. He acted as sort of romantic funnel (sounds rather rude), pulling together all the ideas and squeezing them out toothpaste-like as one united concept.

He did, however, trash most of the thinkers that had gone before him. Generally, he maintained, they had been beating their heads against brick walls by trying to set up philosophical explanations of the world that would not only work when stumbled upon, but once established, would last for ever.

Hegel was sure that human understanding can hardly be the same from one day to the next, on the basis that goal posts keep changing every time we look at them. What might be true one day might well be completely different the next for trillions of little reasons. Actually, if old Hegel was right, I might as well give up trying to write this book and take up lion-taming …

To continue, however …

Take a simple idea like right or wrong. Hundreds of years ago, raping, pillaging and slaying your enemies seemed quite a reasonable (and fun) thing to do – standard procedure in fact. Today the world looks upon this as rather unfashionable, uncool behaviour (it still goes on, but everyone who isn't actually doing it, now disapproves). This, of course, makes finding the truth, at any one point, somewhat tricky. Another example ... Even at the beginning of this century it seemed like a 'truth' that if someone murders someone else, the best thing to do was string 'em up, or relieve them of some organ vital to their well-being (head, for instance) – an eye for an eye and all that. Nowadays we frown on that sort of thing (well, most of us do!) and regard it as barbaric. Hegel reckoned that in every aspect of our lives, or in the way we reason, these conclusions are constantly changing and developing like spots on an adolescent's face.

The Greek philosophers like Socrates, Plato and Co. were mostly interested in man and were not that bothered with the universe, provided it didn't get in the way of said man and his mates. Through studying this long-suffering man, they came up with their concepts (often hilarious) of the universe. But Hegel maintained that whatever conclusions they came to had to be right for the amount of knowledge they had and the point in history in which they lived. The same went for all who followed them, be it Aquinas or Anaximander, Bacon or Berkeley.

But so much more was known of the nature of our world and universe when, say, Kant was writing, that he *had* to be, in the great scheme of things, *more* right than, say Thales. And I dare say that in the year 3000 (if we're still around), philosophers will be 'righter' than Kant.

Hegel used *God* as the term given for the whole process of evolution from before the amoeba – to man – and beyond.

God is really 'Idea'. Therefore, poor God, whether He likes it or not, is not yet fully developed, but is growing up with the universe and with man (how nice). Therefore, the most fully conscious, or mentally developed man so far (all applications considered) is the nearest thing to the universe to date. Therefore, man* (even you?) is a miniature universe in himself — a microcosm of a macrocosm.

And where will it all end? Hegel maintained that history is lurching slowly, in fits and starts, backwards and forwards, towards a perfect state, in which each member of the society blends perfectly with everyone else, and his will (or what he wants to think or do) is the same as everyone else's — a kinda world spirit. Seriously, if I believed that, I'd sleep much happier at night.

The most extreme attempt to interpret the universe as far as man is concerned is found in the movement called **Positivism**. The early leader of the brat-pack was a French chap, **Isador-Auguste-Marie-François-Xavier Comte** (1798–1857). He was a bright young student at the École Polytechnique in Paris, but in 1816 led a student revolt which rather backfired and ended with him and all his fellow students being kicked out. He later became the secretary to the famous writer Saint-Simon, but it was later reckoned that because of Comte's greater knowledge of science, and superior ability to put it over, a lot of the stuff his boss got the credit for was down to young Isador-Auguste-Marie-François-Xavier (Auguste for short). After parting company

---

* or woman

with Saint-Simon, Comte started thinking for himself, and this is the result. Comte believed that human society goes through certain stages: 1) the theological/military; 2) the scientific/industrial; and then 3) the transitional rethinking (which he reckoned Europe was in the middle of). This was to be the beginning of the study of 'sociology' (his word) which Comte could be said to have invented. Anyway this, he continued, corresponded with the three stages in the evolution of each science (*The Law of the Three Stages*), namely: 1) religious, 2) metaphysical (scientifically enquiring) and then 3) the *positive.*

At the first religious or theological stage there is an attempt to get right under the skin of things and discover how they tick on a kind of supernatural level. At the next metaphysical stage (which is not much different from the first) attempts are made to explain things in non-practical, non-material terms, or basic characteristics or forces, which Comte reckoned were simply depersonalized gods (how do you depersonalize a god?). At the final, positive stage, any attempt to discover the inner nature of things, or to try to work out the beginnings of the universe (or where the hell it's going) should be totally abandoned. Instead, the Positivist tries to work out, by using reasoning based on observation, the unchangeable getting-togethers and sequences of things that happen (or appear to happen). Got that?

Unlike Descartes, Comte believed that each different science had its own method which depended on the historical level so far achieved. This made him top dog for all those thinkers who were into the historical and experimental approach ... but cut no ice with the 'knowledge-by-reason-rather-than-experience' boys, who attempted to tell everyone else how science *ought* to be rather than how it actually *was*.

. . . .

CHAPTER 9

Kierkegaard, Marx, etc, etc, etc.

Søren Aaby Kierkegaard (1813–55) was a Danish philoso-pher who, having studied Hegel, ended up thinking he was a bit of a wally. Kierkegaard was regarded as the very first **Existentialist** (a philosopher who thinks man is a free indi-vidual responsible for his own development), a term that will crop up more and more. He believed that man was so much more than the 'child of his time' that Hegel had suggested, and that every man that ever lived was unique; a one-time offer, never seen before and never to be repeated (try looking at a queue for a football match, Hegel!).

Kierkegaard thought that all that continual rambling on about history from Hegel, following hard on the heels of all that sissy Romantic stuff (world spirit, daffs and all) had made it seem as if the poor dim-witted individual was in no way responsible for his own life. He also thought that Hegel wanted to put man in the place of God, and that Hegel was completely oblivious to the fact that man, when it comes right down to it, actually judges everything by his own, rather narrow and, let's face it, limited experience. To be honest,

Kierkegaard reasoned, the concepts we arrive at simply by working them out in our heads, or by someone else telling us, and not by experience, are worth not a jot.

Kierkegaard banged on about the importance of man's free will and his ability to choose what he does without being held back by thoughts of reason, or why he's doing it (not much room for God or the Good Fairy here, methinks). We do something, he maintained, for our own reasons, to please ourselves, but more importantly, to be responsible and find truth for ourselves (classic existentialism). On a religious level of his life, man must be prepared to make any sacrifice, or gesture (even if it is anti-social) in order to be true to himself.

As he got older, Kierkegaard unfortunately got grumpier and grumpier, making more and more snide remarks about the German society he begrudgingly lived in and, indeed, Europe as a whole. This, as you can imagine, made him somewhat unpopular, though some say people had regarded him as a bit of a screwball all along.

You might be forgiven for thinking Kierkegaard wasn't a religious man. Not a bit of it! He believed it was his personal mission from God to be a writer (unlike myself) and gave up quite a naughty lifestyle to prove it (also unlike myself). The main stumbling block came with Christianity and with the way God was approached. Not content to go to church, mind his own business and pray his own prayers, he was slagging off the way others went about their faith. For him, being a Christian meant that it wasn't enough just to pitch up on Sunday, be 'holy' for a couple of hours and then go back to sinning just as you had before (sound like your local church?). No way, he cried, a Christian must live the life all the time, sacrifices and all ... or else! Religion for him was, therefore, an entirely personal matter and so, he snarled, it should be for everyone else (as long as he approved). He maintained, as I suggested before, that it was only when man struggles through all the suffering involved in a firm commitment to God, that he can be properly 'religious'.

After Hegel it could be said that the era of the great philosophers was over. Instead of the need to talk there was the need to *do*. It was all very well sitting around coffee bars discussing the world and all its ills, but wasn't it time to work out *what* to do? Along came a man with the famous words: 'Philosophers have only interpreted the world in various ways, the point is to change it.'

Karl Marx (1818–83) was one of the founders and dominant figures of modern socialism or communism. A German scholar, he had precious little to do with what we now regard as modern 'Marxism', as his objectives were relatively straightforward and pretty simple to get one's head round. Although he studied Hegel, the only thing he gained from it was a bad headache and the belief that change was simply a road to better things (an idea I find totally suspect!). Even a society that appeared to be OK at the time, he said, would inevitably give way to another that was better (our latest government? Please!). Therefore, he maintained, if a society based on the idea of private property gives way to one where the community as a whole owns the lot, it can only be a Good Thing (how's about the reverse, Karl?). Hegel had said that the basic force that drove us forward was world spirit. Marx is said to have turned I$^{\partial\partial}$H upside down, claiming that it was only material changes that affect history and not ideology. Basically it was economic pressures and not much else which shoved society in a forwards direction (or backwards, surely?).

To be fair, up to this time economics had always been fairly straightforward. A chap would get rich by making other chaps work for him for far less money than he would receive for their labour. Labour through history had been so cheap, that there was no great point in pushing the limits of technical know-how. Why go to all the trouble of building or buying an expensive machine if fifty hard-working men could do the job for a fraction of the cost? I'm sure even if there had been some splendid machines to help the Pharaohs build their silly pyramids, they wouldn't have given it a second thought when they had literally millions of willing (OK, whip-induced) slaves to do it instead.

Taking this Egyptian theme further: when the said Pharaoh was buried under his personal pointy pile, his eldest boy would cop the lot, so prolonging the us-and-them status quo for generations and civilizations to come. But that isn't fair! I hear you cry. Of course it isn't! What's fair got to do with progress or the price of cornflakes? This is where our Karl came in. 'The history of all hitherto existing society is the history of class struggle,' he cried, much to the joy of the workers.

Apart from the artisan classes, where crafts- and tradesmen worked for themselves (or the family business) on the one-for-all, all-for-one basis, most workers in Marx's time (the Industrial Revolution) sweated for relatively few fat-cat industrialists and never saw the just rewards for their own labour. 'Zis iz no goot,' said Karl.

He realized that throughout the whole of history there had been an unspoken battle between the two main classes – the capitalists and the workers, the 'haves' and 'have-nots' (or the 'have-not-muches'). Seeing as very few 'haves' in history have voluntarily given the 'have-nots' any more than they absolutely had to, a situation developed where one whole class was slaving for another much smaller one. The only way to change things was – you've guessed it – by force (technical term – *revolution*).

When Marx published his *Communist Manifesto* in 1848 the rich and privileged liked it little, especially as it ended with a call to arms of all down-trodden workers, to throw off their chains and win the world. 'Workers of all lands, unite!' The rest is history.

But many philosophers who followed what Marx was saying thought he'd got it all wrong. One such was (or should I say *is*) **Isaiah Berlin**, an English moral and political philosopher born in 1909. He doesn't go a bundle on Marx's idea of history having an ongoing objective purpose or the idea that all our values are ruled – and devalued – by the place and position we happen to be sitting in at the time (historically). Berlin was big on personal moral values and said we must all reject the idea that every event must have a cause if we are to stand any chance of hanging on to our own responsibility and freedom. This echoes what Sartre (see p.120) was saying over in La Belle France.

CHAPTER 10

· ·

Darwin Rocks the Boat

For nigh on 2000 years Christians throughout the world have believed what was written in the scriptures about how the world began.

In the beginning God created the heaven and the earth.
  And the earth was without form, and void; and darkness was upon the face of the deep. And the Spirit of God moved upon the face of the waters.
  And God said, Let there be light: and there was light . . . etc etc.

Genesis, as you probably know, goes on to describe how God separated the land from the sea and shoved plants and trees on the dry bit; how he invented the sun to light up the day bit and the moon to light up the night bit. Then he suddenly thought of fish to put in the deep, which was all very nice, and then everything that 'creepeth' upon the earth (tree frogs to traffic wardens). This took about six days (with overtime), and when it was done God sat back and thought that there had better be some fab species to put in charge of it all. He'd

made this rather nice garden in somewhere called Eden*
where he decided to put his first *man*, who he called Adam.
God told him he could eat everything in the garden except for
this special tree – the 'tree of the knowledge of good and evil'.
One night when the Lord's lad was asleep, God carefully
removed one of his ribs and made it into this nice-looking
(nude) lady called Eve. But also lurking in the garden was this
talking snake which told her, mischievously, that she could eat
everything, *including* the special tree. Not being particularly
into eating trees, she plucked an apple and shared it with her
new boyfriend. God was well miffed and told Adam off for
disobeying him. Adam blamed his girl (as men have done ever
since) and she blamed the sneaky serpent who looked a trifle
sheepish (or snakish). God then tore the snake off a strip and
said that from now on it could only travel around on its belly
(so what was it doing before?) and eat dust. Then he turned
to the poor misinformed Eve and told her that from now on
Adam should rule over her (many women believe that's where
the trouble started) and that she (with Adam's help) should
start the human race.

And then along came **Charles Darwin** (1809–82).
Though by no means a philosopher, any book about the history of thought would be about as useful as a
joke with the middle bit missing, if it didn't
mention the man whose discoveries changed
the path of scientific thinking.

---

* All my attempts to find Eden have been fruitless; unless it refers to the
town near Salt Lake City, Utah (which would make us all Mormons), or
even less probable, Eden Park in Croydon.

Young Charles was born in Shrewsbury and studied medicine at Edinburgh and then Cambridge. He became dead famous as, during his lifetime, he was to cause a great deal of fuss with his findings and writings. Darwin was a typical naturalistic scientist who supposed mankind to be nothing more than a part of nature. Any conclusions that the natural scientist came to wouldn't even consider the intervention of God, or anything else that came from outside of scientific research. Darwin was the first person to rubbish all doubts that man or womankind didn't suddenly arrive by space craft, magic spell or spring from Adam's rib. Darwin's man was the result of biological evolution. It's interesting to note that Karl Marx went along with this because, philosophically speaking, Darwin's findings in no way trod on his toes.

The boy Darwin had been a typically inquisitive, muddy-kneed little varmint, always filling jam-jars with insects, birds' eggs, frog spawn and sticklebacks, and hardly ever sticking his head into books. He was certainly no swot.

He was sent at first to study theology at Cambridge mostly because his mum and dad wanted a priest in the family, but he later switched to medicine. As soon as his education was over in 1831, he high-tailed it up to North Wales to grub around fossils and rock strata to get some angle on how the world began. His big break came in the same year when he was invited to go on a boat trip to South America (no mean journey in those days). The expedition was merely to survey the southern coast, but they thought it might be quite groovy to have a naturalist aboard, to check out all the bugs and things.

Just like a journey on British Rail or the M25, the HMS *Beagle* took two and a half times longer than the two years planned, but when you think that our Charles' findings were to revolutionize and redirect the whole course of science it doesn't seem quite so bad. As it turned out, being stuck on a boat for five years enabled him to study the minutest details and differences in a host of creatures. It's not every day you come back from a boat trip knowing more about the history of all living things than any man has known before. His feat was even more remarkable when one considers that the poor crew probably had to eat half the specimens he'd caught when they'd finished their sandwiches.

He was only twenty-seven when he got home, having completely run out of clean underwear, but by that time it had dawned on him just how revolutionary his Theory of Evolution was (and how much of a fuss it might cause). He suggested that all vegetables and animals from carrots to camels had 'grown up' from more primitive life forms, and that the process was still going on.

This, of course, not only made scientists sit up and pay attention, and philosophers lean over their shoulders inquisitively, but it caused churchmen to get their vestments in a right twist over its bold implications. If this young

 upstart was right (and could prove it), all that Adam and Eve stuff (not to mention Noah) was more than a little out of date and, come to that, so was a lot of the philosophical hocus-pocus described earlier (please ignore chapters 1–9).

As for this *evolution* business, Darwin's theories were not totally original. Even his own grand-dad, Erasmus Darwin, had suggested as much. The trouble was that young Charlie's predecessors couldn't get their heads round the whys and wherefores of how it had all come about, which had always been a bit of a bonus for the churchmen who'd been chewing their manicured nails nervously on the sidelines for years.

But Darwin didn't have *all* the answers at first. He realized that no two plants, animals or people were identical, and that some sort of natural selection had to take place ... but how? He got the answer from an essay from, would you believe, a dead clergyman, **Thomas Malthus** (1766–1834). Malthus had observed that man was in severe danger of breeding too fast and that the rate that the world population was ballooning was out of proportion to the increase of grub grown. This, Malthus thought, was not particularly good for fairly obvious reasons. Only two things could affect this – stopping people getting born, or increasing the death rate. OK, disease, war, famine and careless driving could at best keep the population steady (but increasingly hungry), so unless people could be persuaded to read a good book more often at bedtime, or spend more money at the chemists, it would eventually end in disaster.

Darwin thought it was all simpler than this. His *survival of the fittest* (natural selection) argument really hit home. All animals, he stated, multiply faster than nature can provide for them (nosh-wise), therefore, in each generation some have to die before they get a go at mating (see rotten luck in evolutionary times). This meant the toughest, prettiest or cleverest get the food *and* the girl, so to speak. Gradually, through thousands of generations, whether you be prawn or poodle, the best or fittest will survive and the brother or sister with the silly short legs or sticky-out ears will perish. Giraffes will get longer and longer necks, ant-eaters will get longer and longer snouts and policemen will get taller and taller. Short-necked giraffes, snub-nosed anteaters and little policemen will be shown the evolutionary door. (Correction: Evolution took a step backwards when the standard height for policemen was reduced, owing to lack of tall applicants). Given enough time, this mechanism, according to Darwin, could account for the long development from protozoa to supermodel.

> An amoeba named Sam, and his brother
> Were having a drink with each other;
> In the midst of their quaffing,
> They split themselves laughing,
> And each of them now is a mother.
>
> ANON

My problem, however (and that of lot of others in those days), has always been — why did wombats stop at being wombats, or cod cod, unless of course they're all going to be humans one day (this would account for some people looking like fish or some fish looking like people). Or, on the other hand, if all species are fully evolved, why don't we have oysters programming computers, rabbits writing books? (*Warren Peace?*)

Darwin's theory of congenital differences between members of the same species, however, was in direct opposition to that old all-men-are-born-equal supposition, as it implied that the whole blinking business involved much more than just education . . .

....

CHAPTER 11

God Gets the Elbow

Most of the philosophers that followed Hegel found his thoughts too idealistic. One such thinker was **Artur Schopenhauer** (1788–1860), a German metaphysician, who endeavoured to disprove everything he said, calling him and Schelling 'windbags' and 'charlatans'. It might be interesting to note that as far as Hegel was concerned, this was largely sour grapes, as it had became a bit of a joke at Berlin University (not known for jokes), when new-boy Schopenhauer organized his lectures to coincide with Hegel's, in order to nick his students. He failed to pinch any, and left the university with his coat-tails between his legs.

Schopenhauer, a right misery, agreed with Kant that the world of experience is a world of phenomena (things happening), but didn't believe in Kant's doctrine of the unknowable *thing-in-itself* (or the reality of something), believing, rather cockily I feel, that he and he alone, had discovered ultimate reality. He recognized man's ability to get whatever he desires. If a man wants a bed, for instance, he can go and get the wood, nails, screws etc. and make himself one. If he doesn't want to go to all that trouble he can simply earn the loot to buy one. Man's ability to get what he wanted, Schopenhauer claimed, was the cause of everything in the universe (and the bedroom). The *thing-in-itself*, if it exists at all, is simply will and the whole universe is a result of just this – a kind of blind striving. Will stands outside space and time, and all reason and knowledge is subject to it. He claimed that man could only find salvation (hallelujah!) by conquering blind universal will, which he thought was rotten and the cause of all our grief.

His contribution was important historically for several reasons. For a start, he was the first major European thinker to reject our dear old God completely. Secondly, he was the first European thinker to be influenced by Buddhism and Hinduism. He insisted on the all-encompassing universality of suffering, but appeared to get more and more pleasure from describing it (what a downer). This might, of course, have had something to do with having spent some of his youth in an English boarding school – enough to make anyone miserable!

Suffering he regarded as essential to all life and reckoned that it increased with every new thing one learns. As for death, he saw it as an inevitability (reasonable!) and saw man simply stumbling along, pursuing his futile purposes (like writing books on philosophy). His statement 'We blow a soap-bubble as long and as large as possible, although we know perfectly well it will burst' simply illustrates what a pessimist he was (and what a bad bubble blower). Like bubbles, he blew away the concept of happiness, since, in his opinion, any wish one can't attain leads to misery, and any wish one can attain leads only to excess (gee, I bet old Schopenhauer was a riot at a party).

Getting deeper and deeper into despondency, Schopenhauer advocated extinction as the final object of a good life, though no one could, for the life of them, work out why he didn't just top himself and be done with it. No way, retorted Schopenhauer, that's far too easy. Suicide is simply an assertion of will, and therefore too much like fun ...

Schopenhauer's three ways to salvation were: philosophical knowledge, involving oneself in art, and expressing sympathy for others. This last one was a bit of a joke, as the grumpy old philosopher was well known for having less than no sympathy for anyone but himself. For a start he simply loathed all women (particularly his mum), any other philosophers and most of all – Jews. He did, however, have a soft spot for poodles and had one called Atma (world soul). Hardly surprising that he was greatly admired by the young Nietzsche, Wagner, the German Poodle Club and a young up-and-coming painter and decorator called Adolf Hitler.

John Stuart Mill (1806–73) was a fairly normal boy who had a bit of a nervous breakdown at the age of twenty, followed by a long depression only made better by reading Wordsworth (which, strangely, makes *me* depressed!). Having rejected all the influences of his dad James, he started writing in earnest in 1830.

Mill taught that when it came right down to it, our ideas are all we can possibly know. There are such recognizable patterns in the way that ideas follow each other, he reckoned, that there is no reason to suppose that they will not always do so. This can be simply illustrated (by me) by acknowledging that the idea of landing on your backside always seems to follow the idea of slipping on a banana skin, and having a bruised bum always seems to follow that.

Therefore the law of cause and effect is all-embracing and universal. Do something, and likely as not something predictable will follow. But what causes all these experiences and ideas in the first place? Is there a universe out there which is responsible for our sensations? If we notice things that happen and situations that seem to repeat themselves, we get the idea that there is something, somewhere, permanent and non-changing. Therefore, he maintained, the external world is simply the probability that these ongoing ideas will carry on as usual. This would mean that there must be some universe, outside our actual experiences and sensations, which causes any ideas we might have. But the only things that we can be reasonably sure of, according to Mill, are the things that we have actually been through ourselves. And we can't even be too sure of those, as we can only make woolly generalizations based on these experiences. Who knows, a set of new conditions could pitch up any day that completely put the kibosh on what we currently reckon to be true.

However, the uniformities that we *do* witness through our experiences can often be acted upon with a certain amount of assurance (day will probably follow night and vice versa). As man is part of the world and the universe, the same factors can be found in him, but the numbers which must be brought into the picture are so huge that any predictions become far more dodgy. You might predict reasonably safely, for instance, that a duckling is going to turn into a fairly average, standard issue, quacking, floating duck, but man, you'll be pleased to hear, is far more complex (in most cases), as everything *he* does or achieves depends on this vast number of factors. Therefore, fundamental principles are far easier to pin down throughout the universe than in man.

For example, scientists, through arduous experimenting and experiencing, are often able to predict with some degree of certainty an event that might happen in the future (a total eclipse for instance). If, on the other hand, you tried to forecast whether a tiny, fresh-from-its-mother baby will be a scientist, rock star or double-glazing sales- man, you'd be in deep trouble (crystal ball or not). Mill believed, however, that should it ever become possible to know all these facts and factors, even these puzzles could be solved. So what? you might ask. What use would that be? Mill claimed that all that stuff we've just talked about, particularly the questions of uniformity and generalizations, could be used when approaching political and social problems.

Unlike Schopenhauer, Mill could be quite jolly in his philosophizing, even though some of his statements got right up the nose of later thinkers like Bertrand Russell, who thought many of his concepts totally ridiculous. Here is one in particular:

Pleasure, according to Mill, is the only thing desired;

therefore pleasure is the only thing desirable. The only things visible are the only things seen, the only things audible are things that are heard, so similarly, the only things desirable are things that are desired. Oh no! said Bertrand, claiming that Mill didn't seem to notice that a thing is 'visible' if it *can* be seen, but only 'desirable' if it *ought* to be desired. Mill may be in a position to tell us what is in fact desired, but he should keep quiet about what ought to be desired – it's all too subjective!

Herbert Spencer (1820–1903) is important as a philosopher because of the major work he started just before the publication of Charles Darwin's *Origin of the Species*, which turned into a scheme for the blending together of the whole of scientific knowledge based on the theory of evolution (ambitious or what?). Unlike our hero Darwin, however, he wouldn't stick to the facts, and intellectualized the whole business so much that in a funny way confused the very message Darwin was trying to put over.

He started by saying that the actual things that are shown to us (phenomena) are all that we can possibly know. What causes the things we observe are not for us to know because they come from an *Absolute Being*. That doesn't stop us making guesses about this Absolute Being since we know that it caus-es all we know, our thoughts and everything in the universe. But whatever conclusions we come to are just childlike attempts at explaining this Absolute – or pointless attempts to know the unknowable. All we *can* know is what the Absolute chooses to reveal to us (absolutely!!), and these things that are revealed *always* obey the laws of evolution. Spencer went on to describe the organizations of groups of atoms to make all the various forms of life, all the while going on about a world outside our human consciousness which causes our impressions ... The unknowable, or the Absolute.

Although highly thought of at the time, Spencer's scribblings had a fairly short shelf-life as many philosophers discredited his contribution. So much so that William James (coming soon) talked of the 'hurdy-gurdy monotony of him ... his whole system wooden, as if knocked together out of cracked hemlock boards'.

Now, **Friedrich Nietzsche** (1844–1900) was one clever boy. Son of a Lutheran minister, he blew everyone away at school and by twenty-four was professor of classics at the university of Basel. But Nietzsche's philosophy got him into all sorts of strife, as on one side he was regarded as the guy who anticipated Freud (see p.107) and on the other, the most outspoken of a long line of opponents (German) to liberal enlightenment.

Nietzsche, like Plato, would never have it that all men were equal and believed that democracy was a load of ... nonsense. Not only that, he claimed, but man's gut-busting will to achieve power could be seen throughout the universe. Anything that is more powerful than anything else deserves to win, he maintained. The weak, said Nietzsche, should be destroyed (a little excessive?), otherwise there will be no room on the planet for the strong. You must admit, this all seems fairly straightforward for once (if a bit hair-raising).

Strong people should rule, the weak should be ruled: it's

as simple as that. Slavery, said Nietzsche, should be brought back and women, because they are weaker, should know their place and not expect the same rights as men. And, just for good measure, God is dead, and Christianity corrupts human nature. C'mon, Nietzsche, say what you mean – don't beat about the bush!

Carrying on in this vein, he trashed Marx's communist ideals, by stating that the idea of an all-for-one, one-for-all society, where everyone shares the fruit of their own labour, was daft. Strong people should take the lot, and the weak should be extremely grateful for what the strong choose to give 'em.

'If you're aristocratic,' said Nietzsche,
'It's thumbs up, you're OK. Pleased to mietzsche.
If you're working-class bores
It's thumbs down and up yours!
If you don't know your place, then I'll tietzsche.'
GERRY HAMILL

It could just be argued that he backed up the findings of Darwin (though poor Charles would turn in his grave at the suggestion). To go against the principle of the survival of the fittest was wrong, claimed Nietzsche, and to try to replace it with a kind of forced equality was even wronger. Having written all this stuff, and much, much more, he claimed that he hated philosophizing, and believed that most of the stuff that had gone before him was simply talk, talk and more talk.

You are probably thinking that Nietzsche was paving the

way for Fascism — that he'd support the rather unnatural (as it turned out) selection of blue-eyed, blond-haired members of the master race. Not necessarily. He frequently put forward as his ideal the creative artist (rather than the bully-boy), or the man that has managed to master passion and rise above constant senseless change and develop creativity in his character. The trouble was, although he denied anti-Semitism and claimed a dislike of his fellow Germans, his writings were often regarded as a blueprint for a rather unpleasant little boy called Adolf ...

These days Nietzsche's influence comes from his celebration of the will, and his deep doubts about the notions of truth and fact. In 1889 poor Friedrich witnessed the beating of a horse in a Turin street (flogging a nearly dead horse?) and, surprisingly, the memory of it drove him round the bend. He died in 1900 totally bonkers.

Time for a French philosopher. An idealist, firmly believing in mind over matter, Nobel Prize winner **Henri Bergson** (1859–1941), was worried about the influence science was having over modern thinking. He believed in old Darwin's evolution, but saw it driven by a huge creative force (*élan vital*) rather than just the ups and downs (and ins and outs) of natural selection. In his view, to try to explain the universe in scientific terms left the scholar halfway up the river of all knowledge without a paddle — or a canoe come to that. To fully understand the universe, one must first get one's hands wet, then dive in and experience it by intuition. The universe, according to Bergson, never stands still, but shifts, moves and flows all over the shop. Many people, he complained, try to examine various bits of it as a way of getting some picture of the whole, but this was like examining a pimple on an elephant's bum to try to find out more about elephants (my words not his).

By attempting to put all this scientific jumble into some sort of order, said Bergson, the life force becomes trapped. Man should try to give up studying matter in order to become free and, more to the point, to see the bigger picture. Unfortunately Bergson's philosophy has not held up, especially his spiritual version of evolution. Modern discoveries by those dratted scientists now tell us otherwise.

William James (1842–1910) was probably the most important American philosopher of the late nineteenth and early twentieth centuries. He claimed that all arguments about first principles of being or knowledge could either be settled or dismissed by trying to work out what would happen if you tried all sorts of different solutions. Scientific theories, he reckoned, were simply vehicles to guide future action, and not the final answer to questions about nature. In matters of religion and ethics (the study of human moral conduct) we are sometimes free to make up our own minds as to which of several paths to go down (oh dear!). If the choice was really important, and if a chap couldn't settle the prob rationally, then it was OK by James to follow one's own best inclinations (I wonder if Jack the Ripper thought that?). An idea's a good idea if everything turns out all right. Many proper philosophers would regard this as a gross over-simplification of a lifetime's thinking and writing, and many successful bank robbers would regard this last statement as a bit of a green light.

Another American, **John Dewey** (1859–1952) was one of the leaders of what has come to be known as the **Pragmatists** (people who support behaviour dictated more by results of doing, rather than thinking). He, like James, saw the universe as a constantly evolving, developing thing – just like human experience. Dewey thought it was too much like hard work to keep wondering about the beginnings of the universe or indeed what was out there beyond that star-spangled blackness. Let's face it, whatever's out there, he said, be it a vast brick wall or a cosmic Alton Towers (heaven forbid), will make no difference to us. All that matters, or should matter, is what we do or what our experiences are, and how they arrive, change and influence each other. That, for him, was reality. So, in order to study the universe simply study man; in him the universe comes to self-consciousness! Isn't that a bit like the pimple on the elephant's bum syndrome again?

Dewey was first and foremost interested in mankind and its problems, a passionate believer in democracy and what would happen to it. By becoming a regular member of society, and by sharing experiences, the individual grows, he claimed. And by giving to the overall welfare of the group, he will receive from the group enough to make him a proper human being (a kind of National Insurance?). Having said that, Dewey recognized the importance of the individual: having a respect for human personality was the only *definite* for him and his followers.

· ·

CHAPTER 12

Sweet Dreams

Sigmund Freud (1856–1939) must be one of the most famous and most argued-over thinkers since Thales started the ball rolling back in ancient Greece. This Austrian doctor invented psychoanalysis and just to recognize how clever he was, Vienna University created a department for him to be head of. Not strictly a philosopher, Freud's obsession was the human brain and the way what we do now or what we have done in the past affects what we might do in the future. To get to the nitty-gritty of his neurotic patients' problems he used hypnosis. He would make the poor devils relive their bad experiences, especially from childhood, and stated that any form of repression should be faced up to as soon as possible.*

Freud thought that there was an ongoing battle between ourselves and everything going on around us. The more society demands we go one way, the more we resist.

---

*Many critics claim that, in later years, Freud himself 'helped' many of his patients either remember, or worse, fantasize the grim scenes that had screwed them up.

Furthermore, the things we do are often not driven by reason (as Rationalists would have us believe), being far more inclined to follow the naturalistic thoughts (science explains all) that philosophers were banging on about at the end of the nineteenth century.

Illogical thoughts often dictate what we think, what we do, and even what we dream. But we mustn't be too hard on ourselves, said Freud, as these thoughts and impulses are simply the coming to the surface of basic needs. Our sexual drive, for instance, is just as basic and programmed as a baby's need to cry when hungry or wet. These basic appetites and impulses, i.e. the relief from suffering in favour of pleasure or comfort, he called our *id*. When we are very young we're practically pure *id* (hence k-id?). That's why nippers drive you mad. When you get older, society demands you get your act together and control your desire for pleasure, in other words − get real (unless you want to end up behind bars).

Talking of sex, Freud even made so bold as to suggest that even little toddlers have sexual drives, which shocked and upset the respectable Viennese of the Victorian era.

To be honest, if he'd said all that today, nobody would have batted an eyelid, but in a society which covered the legs of tables (quite right too), it seemed somewhat outrageous. He wouldn't take any blame, however, as he claimed to have found all this stuff during his countless interviews (and not, I hope, hanging around Viennese parks in a long mac).

The trouble comes, said Freud, when parents or maiden aunts continually tell kids off for fiddling around with or showing each other their 'private' bits. This, amongst other things, he believed, led to all the many sexual hang-ups and perversions seen in adulthood. This often bogus, always moralizing 'big brother' that hangs over us from our tender years is called the *superego* – as opposed to the *ego* which my dictionary defines as 'the part of the mind that reacts to reality and has a sense of individuality'.

Sigmund Freud says that one who reflects
Sees that sex has far-reaching effects,
For bottled-up urges
Come out in great surges
In directions that no one expects.

PETER ALEXANDER

The next poser tackled by Freud was human consciousness. The bit which we actually use, he suggested (that bit that makes us happy, sad or fed up), you could put in a relatively small box. On the other hand, the bit which we call our *subconscious*, which the conscious dips into most of the time, is almost immeasurable, capable of filling a vast mental warehouse. The stuff that is remembered and dragged out for an airing is called the *preconscious*. Finally, all that nasty, unpleasant junk which we've hidden in the corners of the warehouse, he called the *unconscious*. The problems come when the unconscious takes up too much space and starts spilling over into the preconscious.* Having said that, most people can cope with a

* That's when you start going round the bend.

certain amount of this spillage, but the people we call neurotic (and we all know them) are the ones who try *too* hard to keep this unconscious from their conscious.

But it is for his ideas about dreams that Freud is most remembered. He said that our subconscious tries to talk with our conscious through dreams. He believed dreams to be wish fulfilments. This is more obvious in children whose needs (or greeds) are more transparent, but in grown-ups the point of the object (or 'desire') of the dream is often hidden. Why? Because, even when asleep, our mental censorship is still operating, albeit on a reduced level. In other words, we seldom do anything more bizarre in dreams than we would when awake (librarians are not likely to turn into sex-crazed axe murderers). He therefore maintained that dreams had to be interpreted by chaps like him (psychoanalysts) which, if you ask me, is as good a way of drumming up business for yourself as any.

OK Siggie, here's a good one for you. A real live dream. The other day my son suggested that we get a dog. Though resistant, I entered into the ridiculous pursuit of deciding on a breed (let's face it, a dog's a dog, for Dog's sake). We decided that a German Schnauzer fitted the bill. That night, when fast asleep, I answered the door to a perfectly polite, upright, man-sized Schnauzer in a rather well-cut suit. He clicked his heels and said in a heavy German accent that he'd heard zat I reqvuired unt dog and asked what might be expected of him. When I woke up, and having just been reading about Freud, I was somewhat puzzled. I suppose this dream either meant

110

that what I really wanted was a German butler to dominate (retribution for the war?) or something *far* more devious. Where are you when I need you most, Mr Freud?

[Time for a long rest, Mr Farman. Ed.]

. . . .

CHAPTER 13

Science Rules OK

There had been a controversial move amongst philosophers in the early twentieth century to prove that God didn't actually exist, and science was the tool they used to prove it. **Alfred North Whitehead** (1861–1947) was none too happy about this and tried (not for the first time) to develop some sort of system where God and science could be friends. He came up with something called 'the Philosophy of Organism' in which he saw the relationship between man and God as one of the basic things that makes the world tick.

His approach to philosophy was based on the way he saw his own and the rest of his fellow men's lives. Our lives, as he saw it, weren't just a string of events or units, but a constant flow of interlocking split-seconds. The world, likewise, consisted of a mass of changing inner natures and self-contained beings, not only developing and changing internally but also finding time to make active contact with one another. It is this continual contact (and the results) between these *essences* (the things that make a thing the thing that it is) throughout nature, and what happens to them as they mix with each other while trying to adjust to their surroundings, that must form the only reliable insight into world development – according to Whitehead anyway!

And now for the pay-off. It is the particular way that all these forces have reacted, producing the sort of world that we have actually got (warts and all) that is down to God. Every fish, coconut, kangaroo, daffodil, even football hooligan is part of the master plan, and the sooner we recognize this the better it will be for our ultimate good. One wonders, in that case, whether Whitehead could imagine other universes where God had thrown all the essences into the air again and manufactured worlds with little green men and flesh-eating pansies.

If you were to ask the average man to describe a philosopher, he'd probably say: tall, spindly, beaky-nosed, shabbily dressed, with a shock of white unruly hair. He'd have just described our very own **Bertrand Russell** (1872–1970). He was one of those people who go down in history for being famous for being famous and was remembered more by the *hoi polloi* for his unselfish involvement in CND (Campaign for Nuclear Disarmament) and his slightly more selfish antics with women, than for his philosophical thoughts. He'd come from a dead posh family and in 1931 became an Earl, which probably displeased the Royal family no end (never having had a thinker (or thought) in the tribe before – or since). Everyone accepted that he was a genius – not that many understood a word of what he was going on about – but, quite simply, because he looked like one.

Although his primary interest was the connection

between philosophy and mathematics, he was also known for writing quite racy (and therefore popular) works on social and moral issues. These were not quite what you'd expect from a mathematician. So much so that the City University of New York refused to let him lecture there on the grounds that his stuff was 'lecherous, libidinous, lustful, venerous, erotomaniac, aphrodisiac, irreverent, narrow-minded, untruthful and bereft of moral fibre.' (Sounds rather good!) Having said that, he got the Nobel Prize for literature in 1950, so we all know what sort of stuff *they* were after.

Russell reduced all mathematics to logic. He did this first by reducing all basic mathematical terms to logical concepts and second, by elaborating on a system of logic which was good enough to build up the ideas from which the propositions of mathematics could be arrived at (but *of course*, I hear you cry). His definition of 'number' used the idea of a one-to-one relation: if x is related to y, then no other term can be related to y in the same way and the same goes for x. Two classes (or categories) can be said to be similar if their members can be connected to each other by a one-to-one relation. Then the number of a class is defined as the class of all those that are like it, and a cardinal number is defined as anything which is the number of the same class (wow!). Just as everyone was getting their heads around this he went on to say he didn't believe it any more, but couldn't put any other theory in its place (annoying or what?).

His most famous discovery, however, was that of a paradox, which many thought kicked the whole foundation of mathematics in the teeth. This is roughly how it went. Most classes, he reasoned, appear not to be members of themselves. This means that the class that we call 'men' is not actually a man (or 'women' a woman). On the other hand, some classes do appear to be members of themselves. For instance, the class of all things that are capable of being counted would itself seem to be capable of being counted. But what about the class of all classes which are not members of themselves? Is it, or is it not, a member of itself? If it is, it is not, and if it's not — it is!

If you find it difficult to get that to stick in your brain then it is possibly simpler this way. An Irishman goes into a bar and proclaims that all Irishmen are liars. If they are — then he's not a liar and therefore all Irishmen can't be liars, but if they're not, then he is a liar. This what we call a classic paradox (and yet another confused Irishman).

Russell's solution to such paradoxes, and the basis of one of his philosophies, was to arrange things into a sort of pecking order of types, so that what can be true or false of objects of one type cannot really be said about those of another. Therefore, if a given class is the extension of a given statement of truth, it is a bit daft to assign that truth to another class. Tottering on, Russell claimed that it is not false, but it is somewhat silly, to say that the class of 'men', for instance, is human. Even when a statement of truth does appear to pull together objects of different types, it does not have the same meaning in each case. If you say so, Bertie!

CHAPTER 14

···

Existentialism
(or Why It's All Your Fault)

Kierkegaard had suggested that man was a sad little figure in a limited world, and the German philosopher **Martin Heidegger** (1881–1971) tended to agree with him. He, in fact, went further, by suggesting that modern man, unlike his primitive ancestors, has lost the 'nearness and shelter' of 'Being', so much so that truth is no longer revealed and only a very special privileged few* have any chance of reaching, or maybe recapturing a togetherness with Being. Not only has man forgotten the most fundamental question – that of Being – but worse still, has forgotten that he's forgotten! And that's a jolly bad state to be in (according to Heidegger). The only way of remembering the question of Being (and our place in relation to the blinking question of Being) is to go back to all those old pre-Socratics who at least had some idea of what was going on ...

Heidegger saw man as having a privileged position to

---

* He didn't say who this privileged few were, but I assume he meant him and his mates.

Being (how nice) in that we are defined by the possibility of it appearing as a question (our own Being appears as a question and that *is* our Being). Neat or what?

Although Heidegger didn't altogether see himself as an existentialist (someone who believes man to be responsible for all the fine mess he gets himself into) he invented the term *existentialia* from which the movement got its name. The word referred to the three common traits in common man: 'feeling', 'understanding', and 'speech'. Heidegger reckoned that it was only by questioning our existence (Who am I? Where am I? What am I? Why am I? etc.), using these three traits, that man could get anywhere near understanding anything, for heaven's sake. Only when he'd been through this soul-searching process would man be able to go forward to fulfil his potential.

Heidegger certainly got pretty close to fulfilling *his* own destiny when he was rector of Freiburg University in 1933. His most famous (or infamous) lecture called for Germany to get it together, flex its not inconsiderable muscles, and look to that smart new Nazi Party to show them the way. As he carried on, Heidegger became more and more fatalistic, despairing of the way things were going, particularly democracy-wise, which he tied in with a total lack of respect for any form of nature that couldn't be manipulated by man (and don't say woman!). Some people call Heidegger a 'deep ecologist', summing up an entire way of thinking that is based on getting what you want and exploiting it.

It was almost funny when he was taken up by clever French intellectuals as the prophet of the political left. They obviously missed the point that Heidegger's total contempt for the culture of the unwashed masses came about from a heady feeling that he, his close friends and his country were superior, rather than any great head-in-the-clouds love of the left wing.

Karl Jaspers (1883–1969) was one of Germany's leading philosophers and probably the best-known German existentialist. He was Jewish and not surprisingly was 'removed' by the Nazis from Heidelberg University in 1937 but was reinstated in 1945 (as opposed to being removed altogether ...). He hated the high-flown 'professors' philosophy' of the late nineteenth century, only really rating Hegel, Kierkegaard and Nietzsche. If you are surprised by Jaspers' admiration of the latter, who to all intents and purposes sounded like a right Nazi (and not that popular with Jews), it wasn't so much what he said that turned him on, but his concern with human existence and the fluidity and trickiness of his theories. It is only after reason has suffered a shipwreck, he said, on its voyage to find certainty, that true philosophizing can begin. He did, in fact, recommend tragedy, failure, guilt, Mexican food (not really) and even death as a tester for one's philosophies. 'It is only by the introduction to that shaking up of thought from which *Existenzphilosophie* must spring.' Because suffering was one of the big things in existentialism, and because the whole point was to allow man to get used to the fact that he was almost certainly going to kick the bucket one day, it seems to have attracted a whole host of morbid twentieth-century thinkers, among them, Sartre.

Jean-Paul Sartre (1905–80) who studied at the Sorbonne in Paris became, with Heidegger, the other leading Existentialist. He professed to be a Marxist even after he left the Communist party, always maintaining that Marxism and Existentialism go hand in hand in the way they view society and in their aim to express in political liberty the essential freedom in human nature. Isn't it funny that so many Marxists tended, and still tend, to live in non-Marxist countries which (*unlike* Marxist countries) allow one to say what one likes!

I digress. Man, he said, is like a blank canvas at birth and is 'condemned' to be free in whatever he does and positively doomed to struggle under the burden of having to be responsible for the grief he gets himself into. By trying to deny this responsibility, and so side-step all the sh… shambles, man carries on as if his whole life and the choices he is forced to make are predetermined by all the bum cards that society deals him. In other words, don't blame me guv, it's all *their* fault! But, said Sartre, each man is responsible for the evil in the world even though, now and again, he is capable of heroic action (even horrid folk like Nazis could be heroes – sometimes).

> Remember when you are bemusing,
> And daily decisions confusing,
> That life's existential,
> The thing that's essential
> Is never the choice but the choosing.
>
> CYRIL HUGHES

Man's most important freedom, according to Sartre, is the freedom to say 'No, thank you' when that old temptation comes a-knocking at the door, but he can only do that if he is fully conscious in all respects. At the end of the day, despite every bitter blow life may throw at him, man should be capable of becoming what *he* chooses. This, of course, goes squarely against much current opinion which maintains that if a person screws up, it's not his fault (usually we blame our parents!).

But existentialism wasn't the only philosophical path one could skip down in the early twentieth century. A new movement was growing called **Logical Positivism** and one of its stars was a guy called **Ludwig Wittgenstein** (1889–1951) who influenced a group of clever Germans, among them **Moritz Schlick** and **Rudolf Carnap**, called the **Viennese Circle**.

They didn't want to use their philosophy to understand the world, as had most who had gone before, but more to study our language and the uses we put it to. The Logical Positivists believed that everything we know comes from, and can be checked through, experiences that we have *actually* had or sensed (or at least recognize that we *should* have had). The trouble is, they said, to prove one single fact or truth usually involves an infinite number of little experiences or observations which, unless each is 'ticked off', means that we can never really be totally sure of anything (sound familiar?). Simplistically, it's a bit like an Impressionist landscape. Thousands of dabs of colour that mean nothing on their own but when viewed all together (and, hopefully, in the right place) go to make up an image that finally makes sense.

Audacious stuff! But they got even audaciouser. They went on to claim that all past statements related to philosophical inquiry, studies of religion or examinations of moral values were not worth the paper they were written on. (Which presumably relegates this book, and thousands of far worthier tomes, to the lavatory department.) Here's an example. If we say that 'murder is wicked', the statement only really makes one observation that we can be sure of: 'murder *is*'!

'Wickedness' (as a concept) cannot be measured, observed, taken for a walk, or anything else. I suppose, therefore, running down that particular path, if someone had said 'Wittgenstein is silly', they'd have used the same argument to dismiss it.

To Wittgenstein and his lads, statements like that, whether they be used in philosophy, theology, metaphysics, ethics or picnics are simply language abuse and therefore meaningless.

Moving on, they claimed that we can't even use the word God, or make decisions based on Him with any certainty, because, presumably, no one's ever seen him, shaken hands with him, or even had him round for tea (though many might claim they had). This whole simple way of thinking has more to do with the actual meanings of the words we use rather than some great philosophical breakthrough, and for that reason (I think) could well have been put straight in the historical out-tray. It's worth noting, however, that Logical Positivism had a profound, if somewhat mystifying effect on many philosophers who followed and thus cannot be given the metaphorical boot.

Although most modern philosophers have turned their backs on the Logical Positivists, most will admit that they were at least useful for putting the spotlight on questions of 'meaning' in language, before stumbling on to questions of truth or lies. As for Wittgenstein himself, he ended up living in Cambridge, in a totally bare room with nothing but a deck-chair and an electric fan for company (that's Logical Positivism for you).

It should be noted here, that the American **Willard van Orman Quine** (born 1908) should go down in history as the only philosopher ever to have a name beginning with Q.

I could leave it there (and you'll probably wish I had), but it must be said that he also became rather famous for what he thought. He had spent a little time with the Viennese Circle when young and having studied their thoughts fairly thoroughly, finally rejected them (there's gratitude for you). His main concern was the difficulty in finding a good solid springboard for any essay or book about any basic convention, means of understanding and/or words and phrases that mean the same thing (synonymy).

In his book *Word and Object*, Quine takes a rather snooty view of the nature of the language which we use to credit thoughts and beliefs to ourselves and others. These intentional idioms which *will* things to be true or false, he claims, have difficulty in mixing into the scientific world-view and are therefore second-rate; quite hopeless for describing strict, no-nonsense facts. For similar reasons, Quine has stayed well suspicious of the philosophical aim of trying to appeal to believable possibilities and worlds in which every thought or proposition has a definite value truth-wise (70 per cent truth, 30 per cent fib). Thus the only languages that can be used for describing the world literally and accurately are, in his view, scientific and mathematical (sound familiar?).

....

CHAPTER 15

Top of the Poppers

Karl Raimund Popper (born 1902) must have been a pretty good philosopher to be taken seriously with a name like that. He studied and taught in Vienna, but thought it wise to high-tail it to the other side of the world – New Zealand – when the Nazis started tapping at the door (think of a better reason for going to New Zealand). His first *big* contribution to philosophy was his rather natty solution to the problems of how to find the limits to the term *science*.

Up to that time 'science' had been distinguished by a method of reaching a general principle or law by observation and experiment (heat up gunpowder, and you'll be sorry), as opposed to obtaining results by pure logical analysis. The problem, as Popper saw it, was that no amount of favour-able observation, however long and tedious, was logical enough to establish the actual truth of what would come to be known as a no-holds-barred generalization. This, he maintained, much to the displeasure of fellow scientific boffins, led to the un-arguable-with conclusion that science (or the bit that dealt with generalizations) had to simply get by with some sort of faith in a 'uniformity' of nature. This made it hard to define with any satisfaction, and certainly impossible to prove without coming right back to exactly where you started. OK, said Popper, so now we know that generalizations can't be proved ... but that doesn't mean that they can't be 'falsified'.

According to Popper, a million black and white penguins waddling around wouldn't verify the statement that all penguins are black and white and flightless, but one well-observed pink one flying past would certainly falsify the statement (amazing!!).

Therefore, our Karl reckoned that falsifiability was the key to all science. To make it even simpler: science continually puts its neck on the block, by implication at least, as to what can be observed under specific circumstances, but by doing that puts its theories into a position to be disproved, modified or shot down like a tin duck at a fairground. Therefore, nothing that has ever been discovered or written down as the gospel truth, in the whole history of science, can be safe from being disproved or revised. And, therefore, nobody can ever, or will ever be able to say smugly, 'This is the Truth about Nature'. In fact, the only knowledge that we can sort of trust is that which has resisted long, hard attempts at falsification — *so far*.

On another tack entirely, Popper disliked the current view that there were basic unarguable-with laws of history that prove that progress is a foregone conclusion (eat your heart out, Marxie).

Hilary Putnam (born 1926), another American, thought all this falsification business pure gobbledegook, saying (rather sensibly, I think) that no theory is falsifiable either, as no theory, just like no man, is an island. They always involve additional assumptions about anything and everything to do with the nature of the universe. If you find yourself faced with a contradiction, you can get shot of either the theory or the supplementary assumptions, depending on how you feel at the time. Just like Russell, Putnam had the most annoying habit of turning everything he thought completely about-face, so who knows, by now he might even agree with Popper — and not with himself.

Although not thought of as a strictly philosophical term, **Post-modernism**, which affected culture in general, had its roots in the thinking of the 1970s. Post-modernism is associated with the almost frivolous acceptance of new surfaces and a superficial style in general, whether it be in architecture or literature. It saluted the ironic, the here-today-and-gone-tomorrow and the joyful, unashamedly flashy, as an almost sarcastic dig at all those who took progress and scientific truth too seriously.

In philosophy, it made itself felt in a sneaky distrust in all those guys like Kant, Hegel and Marx who were always banging on about progress. Post-modernists laughed at the rather idealistic view of a perfect world, whether it came from evolution (is man really getting better?), improvements in social conditions, education of the masses, or the huge 'advances' brought about by science.

Although well cool in his grave by this time, Nietzsche probably was the first to talk like this. His **Perspectivism** maintained that all truth is some kind of truth if you look at it from a particular angle. This perspective could be merely from a human point of view (how bright you are), or may be bound by history, culture, class or even whether one's male or female. As there are so many ways of looking at things, he -maintained that there must be loads of different 'families' of truths.

This, taken to its logical (if somewhat barmy) conclusion, led to some post-modernists denying (objectively) that the Holocaust or even the Second World War ever happened (although the Jewish community and a whole lot of dead soldiers might just have something to say about that).

The Post-Modern Condition, written by **Jean-François Lyotard** (who might also have invented ladies' aerobics wear) seemed to depend on a happy-go-lucky rubbishing of the success of modern science in improving our human lot. He also appeared to dismiss any attempt to find out anything through the traditional structures of knowledge. However, he did admit that although history and law can't give us *one* copper-bottomed description of what went on in the past, they certainly do give us various more or less accurate ones.

Still a post-modernist − but far more down to earth − **Michel Foucault** (1926−84) had a special interest in the uses of science and reason as weapons of power (either by the individual or by institutions) especially when involved with psychiatric medicine and the study of crime. He wrote lots about how Westerners regarded the insane, pointing out that what might have seemed to be progressive and kindly improvements in the way the insane were treated, were simply ways of building up political and social control. He even went a step further and looked at all social relationships, coming to the conclusion that they were all to do with power, and generally laced with huge dollops of sadism. Whether or not poor Michel personally went through a lot of sadism I don't know, as he is no longer with us. Sadly, Michel was one of the first people to die of AIDS.

One seldom mentions Foucault without mentioning another French philosopher, **Jacques Derrida** (born 1930). Derrida has kept people guessing for years as to whether he's a genius or a fool. He particularly gets up the noses of the analytical philosophers (especially the non-French ones) by saying that analytical philosophy, despite the poncy quasi-scientific way it's dressed up, can be practically anything the practitioner wants to make it.

To prove this, and to really hack the others off, he uses a term called **Deconstructionism** (which is now real big in the States). Applied to literature (which it generally is), Deconstructionism maintains that, within any piece of writing, even the very best, there are fatal contradictions which chew away at any point it's trying to make and often makes it say something completely different. Often the poor writer doesn't even know that this fight between text and meaning is going on, which sounds a sorry state of affairs and probably means that the little book that I think I'm writing is (probably) about something else entirely. Deconstructionism, despite seeming rather pointless to the likes of me, seems to fill Derrida and his followers with abject glee because, as you can imagine, given half a chance, it deconstructs itself and disappears up its own ar... gument.

CONCLUSION

· ·

So What's It All About?

I'm sitting in front of my little word-processor, in my little
study, staring dejectedly out of the window. It's a beautiful
clear evening out there in Wandsworth* (and the rest of the
universe, I presume), and the stars must be the same blinking
stars that Eric and I gazed at when little. My last few months
have been spent studying (on your behalf), not only how man,
from way back, came to terms with the cosmos, but where he
saw his tiny place in it. Now, heaven help me, it's time to try
to sum up the whole sorry business.

You've read (and I wrote) how the Greeks started the
thinking ball rolling and how the rowdy Romans closed them
down. We've learned how the birth of Christ kicked off
a religion which dominated man's thinking throughout the
Dark Ages. We've witnessed the clever Italians dusting down
the old Greek books during the Renaissance and their brave
efforts to divorce science from God, and we've seen how
the centre of learning has moved swiftly throughout

*I'm not in the prison, I hasten to add.

Europe like an American tourist on a whistle-stop holiday.

Then came Darwin, who put the cat firmly amongst the cloisters, by claiming that we all came from the same slimy, primeval puddle and not from some prototype human called Adam. Then came all that back-pedalling from the theological philosophers who tried to get God *back* in the act, with varying success. Remember all those Germans in the nineteenth century who made us wonder about *the-thing-in-itself*? From there we saw how philosophy tried to sort out the unfairness in our society, and how it could also be used to justify the ideas of one of the most hideous regimes (the Nazis) since time began.

In the twentieth century, and towards the end of my illustrious volume, came the really clever Brit-boys like Whitehead and Russell, who required us to have a brain transplant to fully understand how they mated philosophy with maths. These guys were followed by the somewhat easier to understand ramblings of chaps like Freud, who endeavoured to use philosophy to stop us all going round the bend (and ending up being studied by Foucault!), and Sartre, who told us to stop blaming everyone else and get on with it. We ended with the post-modernists (well, I had to stop somewhere), a few of whom reckoned they could convince the world that all the things that happened in history – didn't.

But what can we conclude about the whole subject? Has it helped us come any closer to knowing how we humans tick? S. E. Frost Jnr. in his *Basic Teachings of the Great Philosophers* sees the whole business as a huge, ludicrously complicated jigsaw, with lots of little pieces (which are our experiences) scattered all over the shop. We spend our whole lives trying to put these pieces together. And, just like a jigsaw, we do sometimes find a few that do go together and make sense, leaving little patches of 'done bits' which we could call conclusions. The function of the philosopher is to try and join all these 'done bits' together (when he isn't trying to pull 'em apart), so that we can all see and comprehend the bigger picture.

Frost maintains, however, that even the greatest philosopher in the world (applications on a postcard) could never ever finish this cosmic jigsaw. There's only one person who can do that and you don't need three guesses, or a capital G as a clue, to work out who *He* is.

But for me, the history of philosophy should be seen as a huge bunfight. Some bloke proclaims he's found the answer to something, and another bloke shoots it down in flames. As soon as that second bloke is sitting comfortably on the 'clever person' pedestal, some smart-arse comes along and does exactly the same to him, and so on and so on ...

All that we can be sure of is the fact that, as the history of philosophy has progressed, the jargon has become more and more self-indulgent and less and less intelligible. So much so that, as I neared the end of this mighty work, I was spending more time in the dictionary defining each word than I was trying to interpret what they all meant when strung together. When looking at an incomprehensible sentence written by some German genius with a name full of Ss and Zs, we mere mortals believe that the meaning must be way above the likes of us. It usually turns out, however, when deciphering the

133

jargon, that the point they're trying to make is astonishingly simple, and often rather obvious.

Philosophers, when it comes down to it, don't actually do anything much beyond rearranging a surprisingly limited number of these jargonistic words in an effort to show the rest of us dimwits what goes on in their heads. So, I suppose one could argue, when push comes to shove, that's exactly what the whole thing comes down to – words, words and simply more words (and there's 28,000 here for starters!).

Index

Also by John Farman

A SUSPICIOUSLY SIMPLE HISTORY OF SCIENCE AND INVENTION
(WITHOUT THE BORING BITS)

'For me SCIENCE means anything that pushes our knowledge about us further, and INVENTIONS consist of all those things that make living on this planet a bit more bearable. Sorry if you were hoping to find the History of Mathematics within these pages but, quite honestly, I couldn't find a single joke so I left it out.'

ANTHROPOLOGY ARCHAEOLOGY
ASTRONOMY BIOLOGY CHEMISTRY
EARTH SCIENCE LIFE SCIENCE MEDICINE
PHYSICAL SCIENCE PHYSICS TECHNOLOGY

Awful, isn't it? But don't despair! This humble work will deborify the lot! It knocks the stuffing sideways out of science! Whether you're a budding boffin or a serious science hater, as long as you've got a sense of humour, this is the book for you.

'Highly recommended'
Education Review

'Beautifully irreverent'
School Librarian

*'If I'd known what I was starting,
I'd have stayed in my bath'*
Archimedes

Also by John Farman

ART: A COMPLETE (AND UTTER) HISTORY (WITHOUT THE BORING BITS)

If you're one of those people who think Caravaggio is an Italian motor home, or that Botticelli is some kind of pasta, that Gilbert and George were a sixties pop group, and you're baffled by Art in general, then fear not. You too can be an expert!

The author of A VERY BLOODY HISTORY OF BRITAIN (without the boring bits) continues to debunk the establishment· from the days before paint was invented, the History of Art makes its doomed way towards the present day and a pile of bricks in the Tate Gallery ...

'Brilliantly funny'
Pissarro

'I knew it would come to this'
Leonardo

'It's unreal'
Salvador Dalí

Also by John Farman

A SHOCKINGLY SHORT HISTORY OF ABSOLUTELY EVERYTHING

Ever wanted to be able to reel off the entire
history of the world from one big bang to another?
Then John Farman's latest masterpiece is just
the book for you. Ridiculously short,
frighteningly concise and, as ever,
wickedly witty.

'Short'
Napoleon